PREVENTION OF MENTAL ILL HEALTH AT WORK

A Conference

Edited by Rachel Jenkins and Natalie Coney

London : HMSO

i

ISBN 0 11 321516 9

Acknowledgements

Special thanks are due to Bill Lisle who designed the cartoon illustrations on the front cover and in chapter 1.

We would also like to acknowledge the generous co-operation, advice and support we have received from a number of people and organisations including Pam Buley, Donald Goodhew, Dr Graham Lucas, Colin Mackie and Ann Needham at the Health and Safety Executive, Janet Whittaker and Anna Orr at the Department of Employment, Peter Jacques and Roger Bibbings at the TUC, and also Dr Jennifer Lisle, Dr Vanja Orlans and Audrey Newsome.

Preface

This book is based on the proceedings of a joint Department of Health/ CBI Conference On Promoting Mental Health at Work, held on November 13th 1991, and is aimed at health professionals, personnel officers and senior managers who are interested in finding out more about mental health at work.

PREVENTION OF MENTAL ILL HEALTH AT WORK

Edited by Rachel Jenkins and Natalie Coney

LIST OF CONTRIBUTORS

Positions as at November 1991

Sir David Plastow
Chairman and Chief Executive, Vickers PLC

William Waldegrave MP
Secretary of State for Health

Dr Rachel Jenkins
*Principal Medical Officer, Mental Health, Elderly and Disability
Division, Department of Health*

Sir John Banham
Director General, CBI

Professor Tom Cox
University of Nottingham

Sue Cox
Loughborough University of Technology

Dr Peter Warr
University of Sheffield

Dr Michael Reddy
Managing Director, Independent Counselling Advisory Service

Dr Doreen Miller
Chief Medical Officer, Marks and Spencer PLC

Dr Richard Welch
Chief Medical Advisor, The Post Office

Noreen Tehrani
Specialist Counsellor, The Post Office

Duncan Nichol
Chief Executive, NHS

Alan Bacon
Assistant Secretary, Department of Health

Roslyn Taylor
The Taylor-Clarke Partnership

Sir John Cullen
Chairman of the Health and Safety Commission

Foreword by Sir David Plastow, Chairman and Chief Executive, Vickers PLC

I am delighted to write the foreword to this publication which is based on a historic CBI/Department of Health Conference on Promoting Mental Health at Work. Addressed are the problems of ill health at work, and it proposes steps which employers can take to reduce the costs of mental ill health to business. It includes contributions from some of the most senior spokesmen and women for industry, health and Government which reflects the importance now accorded to this issue. It also publicises the results of a CBI national survey on the cost of mental illness to business.

Why do we need a publication on mental health at work? Firstly, the cost of absence from work because of psychological or emotional problems is enormous. However, even more important, I believe that for far too long we as individuals, as well as business, have been afraid to talk openly about psychological problems.

It is not only the fear of the unknown, it is the fear of confronting our own anxieties about ourselves. We all – at times – suffer mental stress. But while we will nearly always admit to physical complaint, we tend to keep our mental state to ourselves – sadly to everyone's cost.

Time off work with stress-related illness is estimated to have increased by 500% since the mid-1950s and now costs industries hundreds of millions of pounds a year. These estimates do not measure for instance the enormous effects on British Industry of the related problems of drug and alcohol misuse.

So first and foremost we must be prepared to talk about mental health. Not just at a conference – extremely valuable though they are in spreading the word – but also at our own work place.

We must gain the confidence to talk about pressure, stress and strain. And about mental breakdowns – or whatever we call it –

when that most powerful of *all* our tools – the human mind – begins to misfunction.

We know repetitive stress injury happens just as much to people's minds as it does to people's muscles and bones. Why not discuss it openly instead of in hushed tones? Absenteeism, low morale, low efficiency, are all symptoms of our unwillingness or inability to grapple with the psychological problems of people at work.

So there is much to be done in educating the whole country in how to deal more effectively with mental health problems. And, there is without doubt a role that the Government can play in this – psychiatric medicine is *still* the Cinderella speciality of our health system.

Much has been done and is being done to improve this situation. But if you think that the waiting list for some minor operations is bad, try finding out what the waiting time is for psychiatric treatments such as psychotherapy.

However, Government help is a minor plus point compared with what each of us can do, on our own, to improve mental health at work. We must first of all learn to be more sympathetic and less frightened about psychological problems in others. We must learn to be prepared to *ask* people about why they are not happy and to listen more sympathetically.

I will finish with one key thought. The best thing we can do – after reading this book – is to go out and listen to those around us – and indeed hope that they will listen to us.

If we do that we will make a massive contribution to British industry and, more importantly, the health and happiness of our own lives.

INTRODUCTION

William Waldegrave

I am delighted to have the opportunity to speak to you. This Conference looks at a vitally important yet often neglected subject. Let me start with some statistics:

- *First*, at least *6 million people* in the UK suffer from some form of mental illness in the course of a year. That is one in ten of the whole population. Mental illness is as common as heart disease and three times as common as cancer;

- *Second*, virtually all mental illness occurs in the adult population. The great majority of those affected are in the 16–64 age range – in other words, the *working population*;

- *Third*, in 1989/90, *80 million working days* were lost due to sickness absence certified as mental illness. In comparison, strikes accounted only for 4 million lost days;

- The price is enormous. Mental illness is directly costing UK business and industry over £3.7 billion each year in terms of working days lost. The figure does not include any consequential loss of business or loss of recruitment and training costs;

- The total cost of mental illness to the nation, including the cost to the NHS, was over £6.8 billion in 1989, the latest year for which we have figures.

These figures give some idea of the scale of the problem and the burden mental illness places on society – and on business and industry. Mental illness affects you as industrial and business employers and managers. It is of great concern to me – because of my responsibility for the nation's health, obviously, but also because of my responsibility for the largest employer in the country, the NHS. Duncan Nichol, the NHS Chief Executive, writes in chapter 8 on managing mental health problems in a large workforce.

My task as Secretary of State is to improve people's health. To achieve this we need to promote good health as well as provide

NHS health care when people fall ill. We also need a clear understanding of the main threats to good health and the areas where there is greatest potential for progess. Good health cannot be achieved by Government dictat or NHS hard work alone. It needs the active involvement of business and industry, trades unions, schools, and the voluntary sector. Most important of all, this alliance needs to include the individual, well informed on health issues and committed to a healthy lifestyle.

Health of the Nation

Effective alliances need shared goals, and that is one of the aims of our proposed national Health Strategy. We set out our proposals in our Health of the Nation Green Paper in June 1991*. The strategy will list a range of health priorities – areas which are major causes of premature death and avoidable ill-health and for which effective, therapeutic interventions are available. Mental health is one of our proposed priorities.

The health strategy will also propose targets for improvements in our health record. Targets give us something tangible at which to aim; they help engender a sense of purpose; and they provide a benchmark against which progress can be measured.

The Health of the Nation Green Paper has been the subject of an extensive consultation exercise, so that we can reach as wide a consensus as possible on the way forward. During consultation we asked about the key areas to be included in the strategy; the targets which should be set and what they might be; whether those we have suggested are ambitious enough; and how we can achieve what we have set out to do. We have received an enormous number of responses, many of which are from industry and commerce. Representatives from industry also participated in a Wider Issues Working Group, chaired by Virginia Bottomley, which worked to ensure there is a shared commitment to the strategy.

Role of the occupational health service

The Green Paper is in part a response to the World Health Organisation's European Strategy 'Health for All by the Year 2000'. One of the WHO targets is that 'by 1995, people of the

---

* The Government has subsequently followed up the Green Paper with a White Paper[2], published in July 1992.

region should be effectively protected against work-related health risks'. It states that 'the achievement of this target will require the introduction of appropriate occupational health services to cover the needs of all workers'.

The UK has a long way to go to meet this target. A survey by the Employment Medical Advisory Service in 1985 showed that over 75 per cent of the firms surveyed had no occupational health service other than the statutory requirement of first aid. Less than half the working population has access to occupational health facilities. It is hardly surprising that companies have made little progess on policies to protect and promote the psychological health of the workforce.

Occupational health services can make a great difference to health in the workplace. They promote the physical and psychological health of the workforce. An effective service can contribute significantly to the efficiency and the morale of an organisation.

The workplace is a natural target for preventive and remedial action since it is there that people spend about one third of their waking hours. Severe mental illness is fairly rare – pre-employment screening generally selects out individuals who are chronically mentally disabled. Minor psychiatric morbidity in the form of depression and anxiety are the commonest disorders. Set against the cost of 80 million working days lost due to mental illness, alone, successful intervention in the workplace obviously has the potential to be highly cost-effective.

Traditionally, occupational health services have been *reactive*, responding to physical ailments as they occur. We need to develop a more *proactive* approach. Prevention rather than cure should be the watchword. That means keeping a watch – without prying – on employees' health and on their working environment. It means pushing for changes in working practice, where necessary, to protect workers' health. This is good economic sense. A healthy workforce is an effective workforce.

For too long health has been regarded as peripheral to the interests of business and industry. At board meetings, it has featured, if at all, as a perennial entry under 'any other business'. We need to take health in the workplace seriously. Every company should have a health strategy which carries the commitment of senior management. Occupational health services will only be successful if they operate as part of the mainstream of the organisation and are recognised by the entire workforce. For management, they should be an asset; for workers, a resource which they can use to resolve problems and difficulties and seek advice and guidance *without* detriment to their jobs, careers and prospects.

Changing Attitudes

Business and industry need to give greater priority to improving health in the workplace and throughout the workforce. When it comes to mental illness, companies need to work to change attitudes as well as provide services. If someone at work is known to have cancer or heart disease, everyone rallies round. If they come back to work, they attract sympathy and support.

However, the reality is that mental illness still has a stigma attached to it. People who have suffered mental illness can find themselves discriminated against. Ancient prejudices are still to be found in the 20th century workplace. Companies have an important task in telling people the truth about mental illness as well as helping to prevent it.

Industry and business is changaing fast. In common with the rest of Europe, we are seeing an enormous growth in the numbers of people in the service sector. This has resulted in less industrial disease and hazard, but more stress-related disorders. Information technology is producing *instant* working practices. Matters which used to take several days or even weeks are now resolved immediately. Computers, faxes and teleconferences allow immediate retrieval, analysis, transfer and discussion of information. The world has become a global office.

The rate of change is accelerating. Next year – 1992 – sees the abolition of trade barriers in the European Community. This will be eventually extended to include the seven EFTA countries in the new European Economic Area. Change can be stressful. As business and industry seeks to adapt to rapidly changing practices, markets and technologies, mental health problems are likely to increase. Change exposes individuals who are on the borderline of coping. Approximately 20% of the workforce at any given time face personal problems, such as marital breakdown, divorce, or financial problems. Additional pressures at work can push them over the edge.

Treating mental health in the workplace as a serious issue can help prevent breakdowns and illness which carry a high cost for the individual *and* a high cost for the company. It will also support the NHS. Mental health services account for up to a fifth of all NHS expenditure. A significant proportion of this cost is spent on treating and caring for problems generated by or exacerbated in the workplace.

I am concerned that the NHS provides quality and value-for-money. This principle can be applied equally to occupational health schemes. Explicit outcome targets and effective monitoring will help ensure that the costs of establishing an occupational health service can be recovered in terms of improved work performance, reduced absenteeism and labour turnover, a more healthy workforce, and generally improved morale.

We are playing our part in promoting mental health at work. The collaboration between the Department of Health and the CBI and other organisations is now 3 years old. We have several initiatives on the go.

(i)   There is the informal working group on Mental Health at Work. This includes representatives from the CBI, the Departments of Health and Employment and the Health and Safety Executive. It is now a formal sub-committee of the Occupational Health Advisory Committee and the membership has been broadened to include representatives from the TUC, the Health Education Authority, the Welsh and Scottish Offices and ACAS. The sub-committee's aims are to collect information on mental health problems at work and to develop a health and safety strategy in the mental health field tailored to the needs of industry.

(ii)   The Department of Health funded a CBI survey to examine what industry does at present to prevent, detect and manage mental illness at work, and what needs there are in this area. This information will establish the scale of the problem and will provide the basis for future initiatives. Your Director General will report on the results of the survey later this morning.

(iii)   in conjunction with the survey, a joint CBI/DH leaflet on 'Promoting Mental Health at Work' has been widely distributed;

(iv)   Last but not least, we have funded this conference and its publication and dissemination.

I am very pleased that the CBI is working so closely with the Department of Health on these initiatives. It is evidence that both recognise the impact of mental illness on individuals, families, and companies. It is proof of their determination to tackle it together.

The Department of Health also helps fund Mental Health Media Council. I gather it has a stand here today. One of its projects has been the production of a video 'Mental Health at Work', part of an action pack for use by business aimed at raising awareness of mental health problems in the workplace. Further details may be obtained from members of the Media Council here today.

Conclusion

We all know that the 1990s will see increased competition in most areas of business and industry. Falling trade barriers and competition from developing countries will see to that. The successful companies will also be those with the most efficient and highly motivated workforce – and that means those which pay due regard to the physical and mental health of their employees. That is why today's conference is important for the future health *and* the future wealth of our nation. I wish you all a stimulating and productive day.

References

1. Department of Health 1991. Health of the Nation: A Green Paper. HMSO.

2. Department of Health 1992. Health of the Nation: A Strategy for Health in England. HMSO.

1

PREVALENCE OF MENTAL ILLNESS IN THE WORKPLACE

Rachel Jenkins

Introduction

This chapter is written partly from the perspective of the major Department of Health concern with prevention of mental illness, and partly from my own standpoint as a psychiatrist and epidemiologist with a longstanding interest in mental health in occupational settings, although my own research in this area has been confined to civil servants, journalists, advertising executives and pharmacists.

Although the chapter is entitled 'prevalence of mental illness', it is in fact going to be broader than that, and will attempt to set the scene for the chapters which follow, and to clarify some of the concepts we shall be using. I want to cover the different kinds of psychological illness, what they look like, how common they are, how long they last, their prevalence in work settings, their causes and consequences and implications for the workplace. Subsequent chapters will talk about prevention.

It always helps to say what one isn't going to cover, and this book is not about alcohol or drugs. That's not to say they're not important – they obviously are. But they have already received quite a lot of attention in industry. In this book we want to focus on the *psychological illnesses*, the commonest of which are depression and anxiety, and which are mostly caused by environmental stresses.

In a conference such as this on mental health at work, several disciplines, both practical and academic, converge, and each brings with them their own terminology and jargon, and this can cause considerable confusion.

The meaning of stress

So first of all, I would like to discuss what we mean by stress and by mental or psychological illness. The issue is an important one for two reasons. Firstly, while stress is a much abused term, with several different meanings, nonetheless in the sense of external pressure it is something most of us are happy to admit to having a little of. As the Independent put it so well recently in another context, the average Frenchman wouldn't like it to be definitely known that he *didn't* have a mistress, and similarly most Englishmen wouldn't like it to be definitely known that they were not under any stress or external pressure. However, by contrast, psychological illness, while having more precise meanings such as depression or anxiety, is generally associated with a great deal of stigma, and most of us wouldn't remotely wish to be thought mentally ill.

So, what do these terms mean, is there an overlap, and, dare one suggest it, should we dispense both with the pride of being stressed or pressured and with the stigma of being mentally ill?

The Oxford English Dictionary describes about 15 meanings of the word stress, several dating from the fourteenth century but for our purposes it helps to concentrate on three. The first is an external challenge (which can be a good thing). The second is external hardship and adversity (which when intolerable is a bad thing). And the third is the internal state induced within the individual by the external adversity ie the *Distress* or reaction of the person under stress. Thus the term 'stress' is being used to refer to either cause or effect, and this is the cause of much confusion in the literature, and in our own understanding of the concept. See figure 1.

We therefore need to emphasise the distinction between stress which refers to environmental demands and pressures on us (what the OED calls external hardship and adversity) and stress which refers to the psychological and physical symptoms which are the consequences of those environmental demands and pressures on us. The former sense is used in academic literature on the causation of mental illness, the latter sense is greatly used in the occupational academic and lay literature.

Good pressure – able to cope

Bad pressure – unable to cope

And the effects!

FIGURE 1

3

What kinds of external stresses are there?

There are many ways to classify stress, (see table 1) but a useful way to categorise it is into the different *broad social domains*, or marriage or intimate relationship; the other members of the immediate family, including children; social life, that is friends and acquaintances, and leisure activities; housing and living conditions; finance and occupation. All these different domains can be stressful.

TABLE 1 *A classification of external social stresses and support*

	SOCIAL FACTORS	
Domains	*Stress*	*Supports*
Marriage		
Family		
Social Life/Friends		
Housing		
Finance		
Work		

A second useful categorisation of stress is by *duration of the event*. Thus we sometimes refer to *acute* life events such as bereavement, or job loss, or failing an exam, while more *long term chronic* stresses would include loneliness, unemployment, poverty or illiteracy.

Social support

However, stress is not the only way in which the environment has an impact on us. *The environment can also be the medium of considerable support*. It is often thought that only close relationships have the capacity to provide support but there is now plenty of research evidence, and indeed it is commonsense that all the different social domains have the capacity to be supportive, as well as to be stressful. The concept of social support refers to information leading the individual to believe that he or she is cared for, liked and loved, to believe that he or she belongs to a network of communication and mutual obligation (Cobb 1976). This support is accessible to the individual through their social ties to other individuals, groups and the larger community. House (1981) has extended Cobb's definition of social support to include

1 emotional support (esteem, affection, trust, concern, listening)

2 appraisal support (affirmation, feedback, social comparison) which is associated with information relevant to self evaluation

3 informational support (advice, suggestion, directives, information)

4 instrumental support (aid in kind, money, labour, time, help in modifying the environment).

Why am I bothering to mention support? Surely it is really only stress that counts? Well the reason is that we have evidence that support not only protects us against the effects of stress but also that it has a beneficial effect in its own right. Social support can have a beneficial effect on normal growth, physical diseases such as infections and heart attacks, and mental illness.

Reactions to stress

Let us take a look now at *the different ways in which we react to stress*. We respond by gearing our body and mind up for appropriate action. However, if the stress goes on for too long then physical and psychological symptoms can occur. Physical symptoms can include backache, headache, high blood pressure, indigestion or even ulcers. Psychological symptoms can include fatigue, poor concentration, irritability, low or depressed mood, anxiety, obsessional thoughts or actions, poor sleep, poor appetite, depersonalisation and derealisation.

When does a symptom become an illness?

In general when it occurs with a cluster of other symptoms, when it lasts more than a couple of weeks and when it is interfering with normal daily activities. As you will appreciate there is a gradation of health into illness and it is easy to argue about the precise demarcation or threshold. Taking blood pressure as an example, there is a continuous distribution of blood pressure through the general population, and the graph of population versus BP looks something like this. (see figure 2)

FIGURE 2 *The distribution of blood pressure in the general adult population*

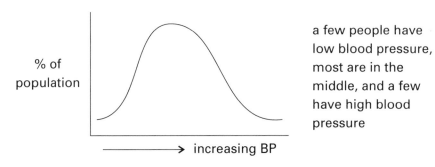

% of population

a few people have low blood pressure, most are in the middle, and a few have high blood pressure

→ increasing BP

Most of us fall within the middle area, and it is a manmade decision when we decide to call high blood pressure abnormal.

On this graph, we can substitute a number of other physical variables or symptoms eg blood cholesterol, or breathlessness, cough, or we can substitute psychological symptoms such as poor concentration, fatigue, irritability and low mood.

These are all extremely common, and they are fairly continuously distributed through the general population, and the point at which they occur in sufficient frequency, severity and chronicity to be termed illness is again an arbitrary, manmade decision. (see figure 2)

FIGURE 3 *The distribution of psychological symptoms in the general population*

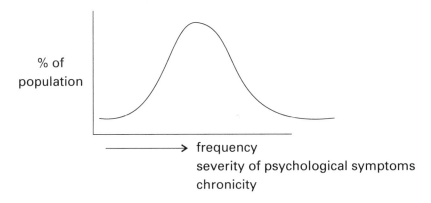

% of population

→ frequency
severity of psychological symptoms
chronicity

You may be familiar with studies comparing average scores on depression questionnaires. These are very helpful as a relative guide to stressful occupations, and as a way of evaluating causal factors, but from a medical point of view, it is also extremely helpful to be able to identify the group above the threshold who can be regarded as ill, in need of support and help and perhaps medication. It's useful to be able to say what proportion of the population have high blood pressure, or a high blood cholesterol, or clinical depression or anxiety.

So how do we measure psychological illness such as depression?

With blood pressure, you measure it with a pressure cuff and a column of mercury; with cholesterol, you send a blood sample to the laboratory. What do you do with depression? Well, there's nothing magic about it, and you don't need to be a psychiatrist. One simply has to ask the relevant questions. You have to ask about each of the common syptoms, and establish how often it occurs, how bad it is, how long it's been going on for, and whether it interferes with daily life. It's possible to ask these questions in a rather random, haphazard way, or to ask them in a standardised, structured way. In epidemiological research studies, we use interviewing instruments that are standardised and structured, to ensure that all interviewers are behaving in the same way (for example the Clinical Interview Schedule which was devised by Goldberg et al (1970)). We train the interviewers regularly, and we check their inter-rater reliability.

This is our gold standard, but it is time consuming and therefore costly for both interviewer and interviewees.

However, there are also quicker, easier methods to detect psychological illness and that is by pencil and paper screening questionnaires, the most famous of which is the General Health Questionnaire (Goldberg and Williams 1988). These questionnaires are not completely accurate. The GHQ has a misclassification rate of 10–20%, depending where and how it is being used. Therefore it is important to back it up with a number of structured interviews in order to calibrate it in every population in which it is used.

So what happens if we use these screening techniques

Firstly in the general population at large, and secondly in the working population? We find that there are some psychological symptoms which are extremely common, and some which are relatively rare (see table 2).

TABLE 2 *Classification of psychological symptoms*

PSYCHOLOGICAL SYMPTOMS

Minor (nonpsychotic)	*Major* (psychotic)
1. Excessive concern about health eg heart disease, cancer.	1. Abnormal beliefs.
2. Fatigue.	2. Abnormal perception.
3. Irritability.	3. Extreme abnormality of mood.
4. Poor concentration.	4. Thought disorder.
5. Low mood/depression.	
6. Anxiety.	
7. Obsessional thoughts and actions.	
8. Poor sleep.	
9. Poor appetite.	
10. Depersonalisation Derealisation.	

The symptoms which are extremely common are fatigue, irritability and poor concentration. A little less common are depression, anxiety, impaired sleep and appetite. Somewhat more unusual are obsessional thoughts, and activities and depersonalisation. Much rarer still are abnormal beliefs, abnormal perceptions, extremes of mood, and thought disorder. Table 3 shows the prevalence of these symptoms in a population of executive officers.

TABLE 3 *Prevalence of psychological symptoms in a working population of executive officers*

% with	Men	Women
Somatic symptoms	13.3 (24)	33.1 (46)
Excessive concern	10.2 (19)	16.4 (23)
Fatigue	29.3 (54)	36.7 (51)
Sleep disturbance	14.7 (27)	15.1 (21)
Irritability	21.6 (39)	26.4 (36)
Lack of concentration	37.0 (68)	26.9 (37)
Depression	28.0 (51)	38.9 (54)
Depressive thoughts	24.1 (44)	26.9 (37)
Anxieties	34.5 (63)	32.2 (44)
Phobias	12.8 (23)	15.5 (21)
Obsessions	18.5 (34)	16.2 (22)
Depersonalization	8.9 (16)	6.1 (8)
Slow, retardation	12.1 (22)	6.9 (10)
Suspicious	2.6 (5)	3.3 (5)
Histrionic	1.9 (4)	0 (0)
Depressed	22.9 (42)	25.1 (35)
Anxious	10.8 (20)	5.9 (8)
Elated	1.9 (4)	0 (0)
Flat	0 (0)	0 (0)
Delusions	0 (0)	1.8 (2)
Hallucinations	0 (0)	0 (0)
Intellectual impairment	0 (0)	0 (0)

The numbers of subjects are shown in parentheses.
(Taken from Jenkins R. 1985a, Sex differences in minor psychiatric morbidity. Psychological Medicine Monograph No 7, Cambridge University Press).

How do we categorise psychological illness?

We make several broad distinctions (see Table 4). Firstly, there are the common illnesses of depression and anxiety, (rather akin to the common chest and gut diseases such as colds, flu, bronchitis, and tummy upsets). These occur in 15–30% of the population.

TABLE 4 *Categories of Psychological Illnesses*

		Prevalence in Adult Population
Psychoses	Affective psychosis	1%
	Schizophrenia	1%
Dementia	Senile	
	Arteriosclerotic	10% over age
	AIDS	65
	Alcohol	
Neuroses	Depression	
	Anxiety	15–30%
	Phobias	
	Obsessional	
Personality Disorders	Cyclothymic	
	Anxious	
	Shy	
	Schizoid	?
	Obsessional	
	Hysterical	
	Psychopathic	

Secondly, there are the much rarer and generally more severe illnesses such as manic-depressive psychosis, depressive psychosis and schizophrenia, (akin to the rare severe diseases of chest and gut such as pneumonia, cancer, ulcerative colitis etc) and these occur in 2–3% of the adult population.

Thirdly, there are the organic diseases which result from permanent damage to the brain, and these include senile dementia, (of unknown cause) arteriosclerotic dementia (from arteriosclerosis of the blood vessels), and the dementia associated with AIDS and alcohol. Senile and arteriosclerotic dementia combined occur in 10% of the population aged over 65.

Fourthly, there are the personality disorders which are life long attributes of the person, life long traits, which are termed disorders if and when they are severe enough to handicap the person in some way. We do not know how prevalent these conditions are.

This conference is mostly about the common illnesses, depression and anxiety.

The epidemiological studies

Most epidemiological work has been done on the general population in the community, and there are now a plethora of good epidemiological studies over the last 20 years showing that about 100–250 per 1,000 adults have a psychological disorder in any one year (see Tables 5 and 6). By far the majority of this is depression and anxiety. Only 1–3% of this is psychosis of some kind, mostly schizophrenia and affective psychosis.

The numbers of epidemiological studies carried out in industry is much lower, and is far lower in this country than in the US (see table 7). However, they tend to show roughly what you would expect, namely that those disorders which are common in the general population, ie depression and anxiety, are also common in people at work, while those disorders which are rare in the general population are even rarer in working populations. So occupational doctors, like GPs, will tell you that the bread and butter of their work is depression and anxiety.

How long do depression and anxiety last?

Research studies show that while half are better in 6–12 months, a third to a half last longer than a year. The longer lasting illnesses tend to be those which are associated with particular social stresses and sometimes with physical illness. (Mann et al 1981, Jenkins 1985).

TABLE 5 *Community Studies*

Author	N	Place	Instrument	Prevalence per 1,000
Myers et al 1984	3,481	USA	DIS	267
Goldberg, Kay and Thompson (1974)	213	South Manchester	GHQ	184
Finlay, Jones and Burvill (1977)	2,342	Perth, Australia	GHQ	120
Ingham, Rawnsley and Hughes (1972)	300	Industrial Wales (Rhondda)	CMI	175
	581	Rural Wales (Vale of Glamorgan)		103
Dilling 1979	1,231	Bavaria, W Germany	CIS	193
Weissman, Myers and Harding 1978	511	Newhaven USA	SADS-RDC	178
Orley and Wing 1979	191	Ugandan Village	PSE	241
Duncan Jones and Henderson 1980	756	Canberra, Australia	PSE	90
Brown and Harris 1978	458	Camberwell, London	PSE	170
Brown et al 1977	154	North Uist, Outer Hebrides	PSE	120

Reproduced with kind permission from D. Goldberg and P. Huxley (1980): Mental illness in the community: the pathway to psychiatric care, Tavistock Press.

TABLE 6 *Prevalence rates per 1,000 population at risk for random samples of the general population for all psychiatric illness in the past month; recent surveys based on direct assessment by standardised research interview*

Author	N	Place	Instrument	Total rates
Hodiamont et al 1987	486	Nijmegen, Holland	GHQ/PSE	73
Duncan-Jones and Henderson 1978	157	Canberra, Australia	GHQ/PSE	90
Bebbington et al 1981	800	London, England	PSE	109
Reiger et al 1988	18,571	5 sites USA	DIS	112
Vazquez-Barquero et al 1987	425	Cantabria, Spain	PSE	147
Mavreas et al 1986	489	Athens, Greece	GHQ/PSE	160
Weissman, et al 1978	511	Newhaven, USA	SADS/RDC	178
Dilling 1980	1,231	Bavaria, W Germany	CIS	193
Vazquez-Barquero et al 1981	415	Batzan Valley, Spain	CIS	239
Orley and Wing 1979	191	2 villages: Uganda	PSE	241
Cheng 1988	489	3 areas: Taiwan	CHQ/CIS	262
Overall rates				164

Abbreviations:
GHQ = General Health Questionnaire
CHQ = Chinese Health Questionnaire
PSE = Present State Examination
DIS = Diagnostic Interview Schedule
SADS = Schedule for Affective Disorders and Schizophrenia
RDC = Research Diagnostic Criteria
CIS = Clinical Interview Schedule

Reproduced with kind permission from D. Goldberg and P. Huxley (1991): Common Mental Disorders – a Biopsychosocial model, Routledge.

13

TABLE 7 *Occupational Studies*

Author	N	Population	Instrument	Prevalence per 1,000		
				M	F	Total
Fraser R. 1947	3,000	Light and medium engineering workers	Medical assessment	283	360	300
Heron and Braithwaite 1953	184	Colliery workers	MMQ			
		Sedentary		334		
		Surface manual		452		
		Surface and underground		522		
Jenkins, MacDonald, Murray & Strathdee 1982	162	Times Journalists	CIS(GHQ)			
		1 month after receipt of redundancy notice and 2 months prior to closure date.				378 (360)
		At sale of newspaper when redundancy notices, revoked, and new proprietor arrived.				378 (369)
		12 weeks after threat of redundancy had been removed.				324 (243)

TABLE 7 (continued)

Author	N	Population	Instrument	Prevalence per 1,000		
				M	F	Total
MacBride, Lancee and Freeman 1981	274	Air traffic controllers during an industrial dispute	GHQ			480
		4 months later				270
		10 months later				310
Jenkins 1985a	184	Executive officers in Civil Service	CIS	362	343	
McGrath, Reid and Boore 1989	171	Nurses	GHQ			270
		Teachers				310
		Social workers				370
Stansfeld, Marmot et al 1991 (unpublished)	10,314	Whitehall civil servants (administrative grades 1–7)	GHQ	248	353	
		SEO, HEO, EO		247	331	
		Clerical		216	252	

And what causes psychological illness?

The very severe psychotic illnesses have a strong genetic contribution (up to about 50%), and we know that from studies of identical and non identical twins who were adopted at birth. However, the nonpsychotic illnesses, depression and anxiety don't have a genetic component. They are caused by environmental stress of one kind and another, and by physical illness.

It's sometimes said, well why should industry worry about these illnesses? Surely work doesn't cause them. Well, we've seen that work is one of the six social domains in which stresses and support occur, and in some people, it is a very dominant domain where we may spend more than eight hours a day, and to that extent it is a potent medium, for better or for worse. But I must emphasise that the cause of depression and anxiety is nearly always multifactorial. There will always be a number of causes operating.

The causes of psychological illness can be classified into psychological, social and biological and it is helpful to think of them in terms of *predisposing factors* ie factors which may have been operating literally years ago to make one more vulnerable to illness, *precipitating factors* ie which precipitate the onset of illness and *maintaining factors* ie which prolong the illness (see Tables 8, 9 and 10).

Again, it can be helpful to adopt a parallel with physical illness. Predisposing factors to chest infection may be a low immunity,

TABLE 8 *Causes of mental illness*

Predisposing factors

Physical	–	genes, intrauterine damage, birth trauma, personality disorder
Social	–	physical and emotional deprivation in childhood, due to bereavement, separation, family discord, chronic social difficulties at work and at home, lack of supportive relationships
Psychological	–	poor parental models, low self esteem

TABLE 9 *Precipitating factors*

Physical	–	recent infections, disabling injury, malignant disease
Social	–	recent life events, eg threat of redundancy, unemployment, major illness in the family, a child leaving home, separation or divorce, and the loss of a supportive relationship
Psychological	–	maladaptive feelings of hopelessness, helplessness

TABLE 10 *Maintaining factors*

Physical	–	chronic pain or disability, side effects of medication, failure to take medication
Social	–	chronic social stress, lack of social support
Psychological	–	low self esteem, lack of expectation of recovery

smoking or allergy or exposure to chemicals. Precipitating factors may be a chill combined with exposure to a virus. Maintaining factors may be not resting, or a poor diet etc.

So you can see that the working environment is one of the environmental influences, operating for better or worse, on the predisposition, precipitation and maintenance of psychological illness. Later speakers will go on to describe in more detail the important stressors and supports in the occupational setting, but these can be broadly categorised into

1   factors intrinsic to the job

2   role in the organisation

3   career development

4   relationships at work

5   organisational structure and climate.

What are the consequences of mental illness

For employers, this is generally an even more important consideration than the cause. (See table 11)

TABLE 11 *Consequences of mental illness*

---

1. Increased risk of physical illness and death

2. Domestic consequences
   marriage
   finance
   housing
   family life
   social life

3. Occupational consequences
   sickness absence
   relations with colleagues
   work performance
   accidents
   labour turnover

Firstly there are consequences for physical health

People with psychological disorders have an increased risk of physical illness, and indeed mortality which is not just from suicide. The risk of death from all causes is twice the norm in severe non-psychotic depression (Sims and Prior 1978) and the risk of death is four or five times the norm in schizophrenia and manic depressive psychosis, excluding suicide (Fox and Goldblatt 1982). The risk of suicide for minor depression and anxiety is not so very great, but for very severe illness it is substantial: 10% schizophrenia; 15% manic depression; 10% alcoholics.

Secondly there are domestic consequences

Psychological illness may cause a variety of problems in the social domains of marriage, finance, housing, family life and social life. Thus those domains are not only the medium for stress and support, ie the causes of illness, they are also the medium for the consequences of illness. For example, continued depression or irritability may place a great strain on the understanding and tolerance of a spouse, eventually leading to marital problems. If prolonged, this may cause more serious disruption of the relationship, and may occasionally lead to divorce, with far reaching long term consequences for children and for the joint finance.

The depressed person may become unable to manage his financial affairs, bills may remain unpaid and letters unanswered. Essential house repairs may not be carried out, leading to further deterioration in the property which could easily have been prevented. Parental illness can lead to conduct disorders and emotional disturbances in the children. Children are usually affected if both parents are simultaneously depressed for any length of time, but usually remain unscathed as long as one parent is well and fully functional. There is a tendency to withdraw from friendships when depressed, thus losing opportunities for social support. All these social consequences form a vicious circle which in turn acts as further stress on the individual, maintaining the illness. On a more optimistic note, occasionally an illness can provide an opportunity to rethink one's life, and reorder priorities, and that can be very positive.

Lastly but not least, there are *the occupational consequences of psychological illness* and these include

Sickness absence

impaired relations with colleagues

reduced work performance

accidents

labour turnover

All of these have measurable social and economic costs, and because these costs may be used in the decision as to whether it is cost effective to initiate preventive strategies in the workplace, I would like to take a closer look at one common consequence, sickness absence.

Assessing the contribution of mental illness to sickness absence

Three methods have been used to determine the contribution of psychological disorders to sickness absence. The first is based on the examination of the diagnoses given by GPs on sickness certificates. These figures are very helpful BUT although high are nonetheless considerable *under*estimates since, like all figures derived from rates of diagnosed or treated illness, they are affected by the individual's readiness to seek medical care for his symptoms, by the availability of medical services, and by the primary care doctor's ability to diagnose mental illness and treat it. And we know that on average GPs miss half the depression that presents to them (Goldberg and Huxley 1991). And even if the doctor does diagnose it, he may not label it as such on the certificate because he is aware of the stigmatisation that often occurs. And of course this method cannot include uncertificated absence.

The second method, used by Fraser and his colleagues during the war, is based on retrospective attribution of spells of absence to depression and anxiety made by research doctors on the basis of lengthy personal interviews with the subjects, and access to their medical records. Using this method, Fraser and his colleagues found that depression and anxiety caused between a quarter and a third of all absence from work in the munitions factories. Such a method avoids the disadvantages associated with simply basing estimates on sickness absence certificates. However, the method is based on the notion that an episode of sickness absence may indeed be attributed to one particular cause, and it ignores the overwhelming evidence from Professor Warr's research unit that most absence is voluntary behaviour which is affected not only by demographic and environmental factors, but also by the individual's attitude to his work, as well as by the presence of a physical or psychological disorder. (Johns and Nicholson 1982).

In order to overcome this latter problem, the third method makes no attempt to attribute one particular episode of absence to any one cause, but rather to make comparisons of the annual absence taken between individuals with identified minor psychological illness, and those without. Using this method, it is found that the presence of depression and anxiety, does make a huge contribution to sickness absence, and that this contribution is greater for certified absence than uncertified (even though the absence is usually certified as due to physical rather than psychological illness), and is greater for duration than frequency (Jenkins 1980 and 1985b, Ferguson 1973).

Labour turnover is another costly phenomenon. It is costly to the employer in terms of wasted training resources and work experience. It is costly to the individual in terms of disrupted career pattern, attendant social disruptions such as loss of colleagues, a break in income, insecurity for the family, and the risk of unemployment. Attempts to understand the causes of labour turnover have largely concentrated on the relation between occupational attitudes and labour turnover (Porter and Steers, Telaachi, Pettman), but there are a few studies suggesting that there is a link between mental health and labour turnover. My own study of civil servants showed that the psychological symptoms score was twice as high in men and women who subsequently left the organisation within the next twelve months than in those who stayed. Mental health was just as important as occupational attitudes in predicting labour turnover (Jenkins 1985c). So it would seem that there are definite advantages to treating psychological illness fast before it results in these costly consequences.

Conclusion

I started this chapter by identifying the paradox that we are all a little proud of pressure or stress but that we are ashamed of psychological illness. I would like to submit to you that both are inappropriate responses. *Taking pride* in the pressure or stress in our lives may prevent us from taking action to reduce it either for ourselves or our colleagues, and to increase our support, before the stress results in illness.

Similarly, *being ashamed* of depression and anxiety may also prevent us from seeking to help treat it as fast as possible. We will all experience it at some time or another. Rather, we need to take pride in our ability to minimise our stresses, mobilise our supports, and to seek help for ourselves or our colleagues if and when it is needed.

References

Bebbington P., Hurry J., Tennant C., Sturt E. and Wing J. (1981). Epidemiology of mental disorders in Camberwell. Psychological Medicine 11, 561–581.

Brown G. W. and Harris T. (1978). *Social origins of depression.* A study of psychiatric disorder in women. London: Tavistock Press.

Cherniss C. (1980). *Staff burnout: Job Stress in the Human Services.* Beverley Hills, California. Sage Publications.

Cheng T. A. (1988). A community study of minor psychiatric morbidity in Taiwan. *Psychological Medicine* **18**, 953–968.

Cobb S. (1976). Social support as a Moderator of Life Stress. *Psychosomatic Medicine* **38**, 300–314.

Dilling H. (1980). Psychiatry and primary health services: results in a field survey. Acta Psychiatrica *Scandinavica Supplement* **No 285**, 62, 15–22.

Duncan Jones P. and Henderson P. (1978). The use of a two stage design in a prevalence survey. *Social Psychiatry*, **13**, 231–237.

Ferguson D. (1973). A study of neurosis and occupation. *British Journal of Industrial Medicine* **30**, 187–198.

Finlay-Jones R. and Burvill P. (1977). The prevalence of minor psychiatric morbidity in the community. *Psychological Medicine* **7**, 474–489.

Fox A. J. and Goldblatt P. O. (1982). *Longitudinal Study – Sociodemographic Mortality Differential LS No 1, 1971–1975.* London HMSO.

Jenkins R. (1985a). Sex differences in minor psychiatric morbidity. *Psychological Medicine Monograph No 7*, Cambridge University Press.

Jenkins R. (1985b). Minor psychiatric morbidity in employed young men and women, and its contribution to sickness absence. *British Journal of Industrial Medicine* **42**, 147–154.

Jenkins R. (1985). Minor Psychiatric Morbidity and Labour Turnover. *British Journal of Industrial Medicine* **42**, 534–539.

Jenkins R. (1980). Preliminary Communication: minor psychiatric morbidity in employed men and women and its contribution to sickness absence. *Psychological Medicine* **10**, 751–757.

Jenkins R., Macdonald A., Murray J. and Strathdee G. (1982). Minor psychiatric morbidity and the threat of redundancy in a professional group. *Psychological Medicine* **12**, 799–807.

Jenkins R., Mann A. H. and Belsey E. (1981). Design and use of a short interview to assess social stress and support in research and clinical settings. *Social Science and Medicine 15E*, **3**, 195–203.

Johns G. and Nicholson N. (1982). *The meanings of absence: new strategies for theory and research In Research in Organisational Behaviour.* Eds B. M. Slaur and L. L. Cummings. Greenwich: CTJAI Press.

MacBride A., Lancee W. and Freeman S. (1981). The psychosocial Impact of a Labour Dispute. *Journal of Occupational Psychology* **54**, 125–133.

Mann A. H., Jenkins R. and Belsey E. (1981). The twelve month outcome of patients with neurotic illness in general practice. *Psychological Medicine* **11**, 535–550.

Mavreas V., Beis A., Mouijias A., Rigeni F. and Lyketsas G. (1986). Prevalance of psychiatric disorders in Athens: A community study. *Social Psychiatry* **21**, 172–181.

McDermott D. (1984). Professional Burnout and its relation to job characteristics, Satisfaction and Control. *Journal of Human Stress* 79–85.

McGrath A., Reid N. and Boore J. (1989). Occupational Stress in Nursing. *International Journal of Nursing Studies* **26**, 343–358.

Myers J. K., Weissman M. M., Tischler G. L. et al (1984). Six month prevalence of psychiatric disorders in three communities. *Archives of General Psychiatry* **41**, 959–67.

Orley J. and Wing J. (1979). Psychiatric disorder in two African villages. *Archives of General Psychiatry* **36**, 513–520.

Regier D., Boyd J., Burke J., Rae D., Myders J., Kramer M., Robins L., George L., Karno M. and Locke B. (1988). One month prevalence of mental disorders in the United States. *Archives of General Psychiatry* **45**, 977–985.

Sims A. and Prior P. (1978). The pattern of mortality in severe neuroses. *British Journal of Psychiatry* **133**, 299–305.

Stansfeld S. and Marmot M. (1991) (unpublished). Whitehall II study of civil servants.

Vazquez-Barquero J., Munoz P. and Madox Jauregi V. (1981). The interaction between physical illness and neurotic morbidity in the community. *British Journal of Psychiatry* **139**, 328–355.

Vazquez-Barquero J., Munoz P. and Madoz Jauregi V. (1981). The interaction between physical illness and neurotic morbidity in the community. *British Journal of Psychiatry* **139**, 328–335.

Vazquez-Barquero J., Diez-Mannique J. F., Pena C., Aldama J., Samaniego Roderiginez C., Menandez Arango J. and Mirapeix C. (1987). A community mental health survey in Canbalima a general description of morbidity. *Psychological Medicine* **17**, 227–241.

Weissman M., Myers J. and Harding P. (1978). Psychiatric disorders in a US urban community: 1975/76. *American Journal of Psychiatry* **135**, 459–462.

2

THE COST OF MENTAL ILL HEALTH TO BUSINESS

Sir John Banham

It is encouraging that the Government is finally worrying about outputs and results instead of inputs and taxes. Some of us were doing that in 1974 when this document on Ongoing Health was published by McKinsey. It set out the most common causes of death and gave some pretty grim statistics on ill health and lifestyle factors. It is pleasing that the Government has recognised the importance of prevention and promotion in managing health and is beginning to embrace these principles.

There are a number of questions that should be considered today.

First, why is health important for business?

British business is not short of worthy targets for its efforts and energies, and when we begin to climb out of recession the agenda is busier than ever. Yet there can be no doubt that health promotion has its place on that business agenda. That is for one excellent reason; Ill health costs business money.

In particular, mental ill health accounts for a significant proportion of this cost.

It is widely recognised that stress is a major contributor to absenteeism and sickness absence. The CBI estimates that the cost of certified sickness absence for stress and mental disorders to be £5.3 billion for 1987/88.

That figure takes no account of the cost of absence that has been miscertified, (few people want a certificate referring to their mental health) or of absence that lasts less than 7 days which is subject to self certification.

What have other people said?

The Health and Safety Executive estimate that 80 million working days are lost to mental illness every year. This costs employers between £1 and £2 billion each year.

Thirty days are lost to stress for every single day lost to industrial disputes.

In 1989, a survey of 200 companies showed that the main factors perceived to be related to absenteeism were poor motivation, drink related problems and work stress.

A MORI poll of 112 of the top 500 UK companies showed that 65% of them believed stress was the major factor in ill health for their organisations.

The evidence seems conclusive. Mental illness and stress will cost business money – but why? I should like to take a few moments to explore how problems manifest themselves in the work place.

Many of the recurrent difficulties in managing people can have mental health problems as a root cause. For example;

Genuine sickness absence – there are two aspects to this, physical illness and mental illness. Undoubtedly stress is a major contributor to physical illness because it lowers the body's natural resistance to illness.

Non-attendance – lack of motivation is a major factor in non-attendance. Other factors include alcohol and drug abuse. Then there are those for whom going to work that day is simply too much for them to cope with. All these factors can be caused or influenced by stress.

Reduced productivity – a stressed individual does not work as effectively.

Labour turnover – Recruitment is a very costly business and stress may contribute to an employee's decision to leave.

Poor time keeping – half an hour late, an extra 20 minutes at lunch, home an hour early adds up over a period of time.

Ineffective working – an employee may be making incorrect assessments, failing to meet deadlines, doing a bad job, perhaps necessitating the work being redone.

Poor interpersonal relations – a stressed employee may alienate colleagues, cause disputes, refuse to take management instruction, fail to manage effectively, offend a client or customer.

But more importantly we live in the era of the catastrophe. An age where it only takes one employee to make one mistake and the most appalling damage can be done.

This is a huge responsibility for both business and the individual. The impact on a firm implicated in a catastrophe can be so deep as to be irrecoverable. Indeed if one explores the link between stress and increased consumpton of alcohol and drugs the potential for a catastrophe grows.

What response is business making to these challenges to its effectiveness?

I have to say that business could be doing more. The response to a problem that is well documented and understood has been somewhat hit and miss.

A recent CBI survey sought to establish what the business community understands about mental illness, and what action is being taken. Companies of every size within a complete spectrum of activities in all regions of the UK were surveyed.

Are employers interested in promoting mental health?

I think the results speak for themselves.

We asked 'Should mental illness be of concern to your company?' 94% of respondents said yes. But of those, only 52% felt that a company policy on mental health was appropriate, and only 12% actually had such a policy. Only 11% have a company programme for managing mental health.

Clearly, whilst many businesses recognise that the mental health of their employees is important to their business, they do not see a need to take action. The battle may be half won, but now these gains must be consolidated by showing companies how to take that action.

The Health and Safety Executive estimated that the cost to the nation of sick leave due to mental health problems is nearly £2 billion. 32% of respondents believed the figure was accurate. 50% were surprised by its magnitude, yet just under 20% of them said they would be stimulated to take action by this figure. Is that enough action in the face of evidence that minor mental ill health directly costs business money?

Perhaps quoting big numbers is not the most effective stimulus for action. The figure for those who would take action was very different when the stimulus was one of their own employees becoming mentally ill. A staggering 85% of respondents said that a problem in their own work place would promote a general initiative. Yet business needs to take action before the problem arises; that is what Mr Waldegrave's Green Paper is all about*.

The survey demonstrated that the general level of understanding of stress, its effects and causes was high. Well over 50% of respondents claimed to understand stress, and the response was only slightly reduced for anxiety and depression.

The survey explored the factors believed to affect the mental health of individuals.

The greatest work place cause of stress by far was thought to be the threat of redundancy. Less than 3% believed that it did not cause stress. Personal problems were viewed as causing more stress than work place problems, with marriage problems rating first, followed by bereavement and then financial problems.

We also asked what was being done about alcohol and drugs. Over a quarter of respondents had alcohol policies and a sixth had policies for drugs in the work place. Both of these are greater than the meagre 12% for mental health policies but still inadequate considering that as long as ten years ago there were over half a million alcoholics in England and Wales and some 5 million who fell just short of the threshold beyond which harm develops from their drinking.

So to sum up the survey findings. Employers recognise that mental health is important and mostly they understand the causal factors, but only a minority are taking specific action to promote mental health at work.

---

* The Government has subsequently followed up the Green Paper with a White Paper, 'The Health of the Nation: A Strategy for Health in England' published in July 1992.

To turn these figures around it is important to understand how work and minor mental ill health relate to each other and the return that can be expected on investment if health promotion schemes and services are put in place.

The first difficulty is that of getting the message across effectively. Consider the challenge;

- do we know who we should be talking to?

- are we in fact addressing them?

- are they paying attention?

- have they heard the right message?

- will they act upon it?

- will it work?

Unless all these questions can be answered yes, then any health promotion activites will not fulfil their potential, irrespective of their scale. Mental health management can be achieved with differing amounts of resource and investment. It can involve major pan organisational systems, with support at all levels. This can be expensive, yet cost effective. There are several good examples of this kind of system already in existence. The Post Office has an excellent counselling scheme, as do Whitbread plc, both clear examples of best practice. Indeed Whitbread's employee assistance programme is now in its third year and has just been expanded to include more regions. The success of this programme and the positive benefits that it has brought to Whitbread should encourage businesses to consider how health promotion can work for them.

In the United States, Employee Assistance programmes are more common, and data shows that the return per dollar invested is between $3 and $17.

Alternately, stress management can be small; sector or person specific with limited support. What is appropriate depends on the organisation.

Ideally, all employees should benefit, whether they recognise the stresses of work or not. It is important to remember that stress is no respecter of rank. The systems need to be as good for the post boy as for the MD.

The main message is that now is the time for action. Business can learn from the experiences of others and make mental health promotion work.

In our current trading world where the customer is King, the only relative advantage available to British companies, at least an advantage that is sustainable, lies in the quality and commitment of its employees. Investing in employees and enjoying the return on that investment is part of a long term growth plan. Promoting mental health is arguably one of the best forms of investment an employer can make. I commend it to you.

Mental Health at Work: Assessment and Control

Tom Cox and Sue Cox

Introduction

Minor forms of psychological (mental) ill health are common among the adult working population, and it has been suggested that the experience of such ill health is related to, among other things, sickness absence, non attendance and reduced effectiveness of personnel. What is not clear is the *extent* to which work influences psychological ill health. For example, is the design of work a contributing factor in the aetiology of psychological ill health or is it an exacerbating factor when problems already exist? Is work a positive psychological health factor, say when work is compared with unemployment? Despite these questions and some uncertainty, it is clear from the available scientific evidence that work has the *potential* for impairing aspects of psychological health. Contemporary stress research has, for example, established a firm link between different aspects of work design, for example the combination of high workload and low control, the experience of stress and subsequent psychological health outcomes.

Conceptual Framework

Thinking about psychological ill health in relation to stress provides a clear framework for its assessment and subsequent control in the workplace. The model can be described in terms of exposure to particular work hazards and the attendant risk of psychological harm (see S. Cox and Tait, 1991). The key questions thus concern:

1   the nature of the relevant work hazards,

2   the nature and magnitude of the potential harm, and

3   the probability of that harm occurring.

These questions are modelled in figure 1 and the key concepts are discussed below.

FIGURE 1 *Workplace Hazards, Stress and Psychological Health*

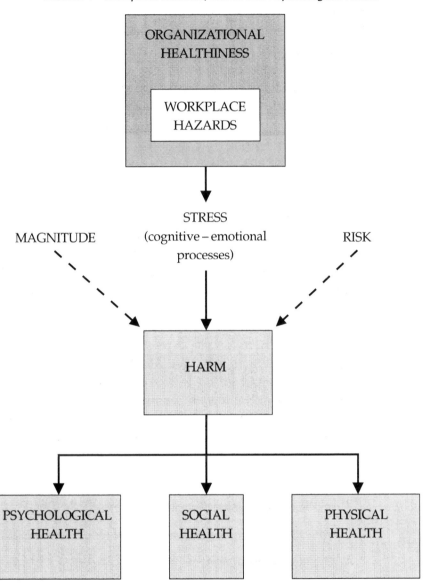

There are possibly two types of relationship between work hazards and psychological ill health. First, there may be a direct link between exposure to certain psychological, social and organizational hazards and such ill health (and these hazards may be represented in aspects of job and organization design). Second, psychological ill health may result from exposure to other types of hazard, such as chemical or microbiological hazards, and *worry* over their possible health effects. Anxiety over hazards to health may be a major issue for a number of professional and occupational groups such as nurses and VDU operators (Cox, 1987a).

Stress may be considered to be one outcome of experiencing problems at work. According to contemporary theory, work demands which are not well matched to the knowledge and skills of employees, especially where those employees have little control over work and received little support at work, represent hazards which may cause an impairment of psychological health through the experience of stress (Cox and Ferguson, 1991). Such psychosocial hazards will be expressed in different ways for different jobs and in different organizations.

Recent research at Nottingham, on the nature of healthy organizations, suggests that problems in six different *aspects of organizations* may be related to the experience of stress and to the psychological health of employees (Cox and Kuk, 1992).

1   organizational culture,

2   the management and social environments,

3   communication,

4   the task environment,

5   the problem solving environment, and

6   the (staff) development environment.

The possible effects of such problems need to be carefully considered and a broad view of psychological ill health taken, one which includes non clinical states, such as impaired job satisfaction, as well as degrees of suboptimal health, in addition to clinical states such as the minor and major psychiatric conditions.

Risk can be expressed as the product of the likelihood of harm occurring and the magnitude of that harm. Several different types of risk need to be considered:

1 *objective* risk as calculated from the available statistical evidence,

2 *subjective* risk as the person's perception of the risk (or that of their group or of society),

3 *relative* risk as a comparison between the likelihood (etc) of harm resulting from exposure to different hazards, and

4 *acceptable* risk as the level of risk that can be accepted for those exposed to that hazard.

Information on the nature of hazards, exposure to hazards, their possible harmful effects and the risks involved may be gandered from several different sources, such as employee surveys, case evidence, epidemiological studies and the existing scientific literature.

Occupational Health & Stress Audit

Identifying possible work hazards, investigating their nature and pattern of possible effects, and estimating exposure and risk statistics are properly part of an *occupational health & stress audit*. Such an audit, as developed by Maxwell & Cox Associates, should also consider the organization's policy for mental health, and its arrangements, resources and organization for implementing that policy.

Legal Framework

There is a legal framework for the development and implementation of such audits and for subsequent risk management: that provided by the UK and European health and safety legislation. The 1974 Health & Safety at Work Act provided the starting point for contemporary thinking about the need for and nature of risk management. The systematic problem solving approach, which is implicit in much of that thinking, will be further extended when the Workplace Safety Framework Directive assessments are required with the implementation of that Directive in the UK. However, the approach is currently made explicit in the Regulations for the Control of Substances Hazardous to Health 1988.

This scheme, and the problem solving approach, may be readily adapted for use in relation to the explanation and management of psychological health problems (see, for example, Cox, 1987b).

Control Cycle

The problem solving approach to risk management for psychological health can be described in five stages as a *control cycle* involving:

1 first, the recognition that employees are experiencing psychological problems, and the identification of the hazards which are giving rise to that experience, and

2 second, the assessment of the risk to psychological health associated with those hazards,

3 third, the nature of reasonable and practicable control strategies,

4 fourth, the planned implementation of those strategies, and

5 fifth, the monitoring and evaluation of the effects of those strategies feeding back into a re-appraisal of the whole process.

It is also necessary for organizations to consider the implications of their experience with this control cycle for information to and the training of employees. However, a key stage in the application of the control cycle is the design of appropriate (reasonable and practicable) control strategies.

Stress Control Strategies

Control strategies, for psychological health, share one of three objectives as described by Cox, Leather and Cox in 1990:

1 to prevent the occurrence of problem (hazardous) situations at work, or to reduce the frequency with which they occur,

2 to increase awareness of such problems, and of psychological health issues and improve the problem solving strategies and management systems available to deal with them, and

3   to treat or rehabilitate individuals (and organisations) who
    have experienced psychological health problems.

Several general points need noting at this stage.

First, it is important that a *total organizational response* to psychological health issues is planned and implemented. Sadly, it is
neither sufficient or effective to simply 'add in' an employee
counselling service. A whole range of actions need to be considered and those chosen integrated into a coherent programme.
Often this starts with the formulation of a mental health policy,
and the specification of the arrangements, resources and organization available to support that policy. Such actions can lead into
a careful review of design issues, of management systems and
practice, and of the need for enhanced employee support. All
actions, of course, need to be monitored and evaluated. It should
be noted that, in the authors' experience, much can be achieved
within organizations by exploiting existing resources.

Second, within this total organizational response *'prevention is
better than cure'*.

Last, it is counter productive (and arguably unethical) to simply
provide awareness training for managers and other employees,
thus sensitizing them to psychological health problems, without
also giving them the tools and systems needed to deal with those
problems.

Questions: Agency & Target

These different types of strategy may be mapped on to three
questions, which deal with the target of the intervention and its
agency (organisation or individual employee):

- what can the organisation do to put its own house in order
  (organisation : organisation),

- what can the organisation do to help or assist its individual
  employees (organisation : employee), and

- what can those individual employees do to help themselves
  (employee : employee)?

What Can the Organization Do for Itself?

Problem situations may arise within organisations because of
failures of selection or training, or of updating employees'

knowledge, skills and attitudes. They may arise because jobs, technology and work environments have not been systematically designed with employees in mind. They might arise because of management style and practice, because of the very culture of the organisation, or because change has not been well managed.

There are therefore three levels at which organisational strategies can operate; in terms of:

- developing the structure, function and culture of the organization itself,

- developing line management function, and also

- developing the function of specialist management.

Interestingly, much of what is being argued here is *organization development*. Not surprisingly, there are obviously many different ways in which the organization can put its own house in order. None are magical or mystical and most are not particularly new. However, although such strategies are a cost to the organisation, this has to be weighed against the potential benefits of increased employee and customer (client) satisfaction, and improved organisational flexibility and performance.

What Can the Organization Do for its Employees?

In addition to taking a long, hard and possibly critical look at itself, the organization can also consider adding something extra for its staff.

A relatively small number of large organizations support a traditional occupational health service, rather more buy into one of this country's private medical services. In addition, many organisations, both in the USA and in Europe, also offer their staff access to special programmes designed to improve their general health and fitness, and help them cope with the challenge of work. These programmes have been given a whole variety of different titles, but are perhaps most easily recognised as *'employee assistance programmes'* (EAPs).

Our evidence (see, for example, Cox, Leather and Cox, 1990), and that of others, suggests that such programmes have several common elements: the provision of health promotion information (usually smoking cessation, weight control, controlled drinking and diet), fitness and relaxation training, group discussions and/or access to a professional counsellor or better still a personal consultant psychologist, and training in coping skills (such as time management or assertiveness).

Although set up and sponsored by the organization, these programmes can only succeed if the individuals involved are convinced of their value and are drawn into participation. They have to accept at least part ownership of their problems. Much of what is on offer can be taken on board by those individuals outside of work, perhaps as part of developing a healthier and more robust lifestyle. Thus the question 'what can the organisation do for the individual becomes what can the individual do for themselves?'.

Stress Toolkit

Sadly, whatever the answers to these questions are for the individual, there is still relatively little evidence available on the relative effectiveness of any of these different strategies. This is one reason why the Centre for Organizational Health & Development has been established in the Department of Psychology at the University of Nottingham. Working in conjunction with several other bodies, such as the Health & Safety Unit, Centre for Extension Studies at Loughborough University, and the consultancy group Maxwell & Cox Associates, it is attempting to identify, describe and evaluate existing occupational health and employee assistance programmes. However, not content with this seemingly academic, but nevertheless important, exercise, the Centre and the consultancy are also offering to design, implement and evaluate new schemes based on their developing knowledge and expertise in this area, and their commitment to promoting the occupational health (and safety) of those at work.

One recent initiative is the *Stress Toolkit* developed by Maxwell & Cox Associates and the Centre for Extension Studies at Loughborough University. The Stress Toolkit is part of the 'Human Factors' programme being offered by the Health & Safety Unit, Centre for Extension Studies at Loughborough University of Technology. It is a practical aid for both line managers and work counsellors and welfare officers; those who have to help employees under pressure as part of their responsibilities at work. The Toolkit is both a system and a package of practical resources which have been developed to help managers, work counsellors and welfare officers (a) to help employees better understand the problems they face, and then (b) to help those employees to build, implement and monitor individual coping strategies to deal with those problems. The system is designed around our current knowledge of both 'helping' and the management of health and stress in the workplace. It is not simply another counselling package!

The Stress Toolkit can sensibly form *one* part of a 'total organisational response' to the problem of stress at work and should follow on from an occupational health & stress audit. It has been designed to develop and supplement an organisation's existing resources as its first line of defence against stress and, at the same time, can form the basis for an employee assistance programme (EAP). The training offered through the Centre for Extension Studies, Loughborough University, in support of the Toolkit, empahsises the need to plan its evaluation when implementing the system, and discusses how the information gained through such evaluation can be used to help both the organisation and its employees. It also emphasises the need for individuals to monitor the success of their individual coping strategies and modify their use appropriately.

Conclusions

This chapter briefly sets out an approach to psychological health issues at work which is based on the application of stress theory within an occupational health framework. It argues that the experience of work stress may be related to psychological ill health and that the demands which contribute to the experience of stress may be treated and controlled in much the same way as the other more tangible hazards of work. A systematic problem solving approach is proposed based on the notion of the *control cycle*. The nature of possible organizational control strategies is then explored and the concept of the *total organizational response* introduced. Finally, as a possible element in that response, the Stress Toolkit is described.

References

Cox, S., and Tait, R. (1991) *Reliability, Safety and Risk Management: An Integrated Approach*. Butterworth—Heinemann, London.

Cox, T. (1987a) Looking Forward. *Work & Stress*, **2**, 109–111.

Cox, T. (1987b) Stress, coping and problem solving. *Work & Stress*, **1**, 5–14.

Cox, T., and Ferguson, E. (1991) Individual differences, stress and coping. In: C. L. Cooper and R. Payne (eds) *Personality and Stress: Individual Differences in the Stress Process*. Wiley & Sons, Chichester.

Cox, T., and Kuk, G. (1992) Healthiness of schools as organizations: teacher stress and health. In: *Proceedings of International Congress on Stress, Anxiety & Emotional Disorders*, University of Minho, Braga, Portugal.

Cox, T., Leather, P., and Cox, S (1990) Stress, health and organizations. *Occupational Health Review*, **23**, 13–18.

Cox, T., and Ferguson, E. (1991) Individual differences, stress and coping. In: C. L. Cooper and R. Payne (eds) *Personality and Stress: Individual Differences in the Stress Process*. Wiley & Sons, Chichester.

Cox, T., and Kuk, G. (1992) Healthiness of schools as organizations: teacher stress and health. In: *Proceedings of International Congress on Stress, Anxiety & Emotional Disorders*. University of Minho, Braga, Portugal.

Further Information

Further information on the research conducted by the Centre for Organizational Health & Development concerned with occupational health and stress, including the nature and control of violence at work, can be obtained from:

Centre for Organizational Health & Development,
Department of Psychology, University of Nottingham,
Nottingham NG7 2RD, UK

Information on the training and development programmes offered by the Centre for Extension Studies, and in particular the Stress Toolkit, can be obtained from:

Health & Safety Unit, Centre for Extension Studies,
Loughborough University of Technology,
Loughborough, Leicestershire LE11 3TU, UK

Information on the consultancy services offered by Maxwell & Cox Associates in relation to occupational health and stress, and health and safety, can be obtained from:

Maxwell & Cox Associates,
Meriden, 10, Luttrell Road,
Four Oaks Park, Sutton Coldfield,
West Midlands B74 2SP.

4

JOB FEATURES AND EXCESSIVE STRESS

Peter Warr

Introduction

Good mental health at work can be promoted by two means: assisting and counselling individual people, or by the effective design of jobs. As demonstrated in other chapters, the former approach is of great value (see also Firth and Shapiro, 1986), but if job conditions remain unchanged we have not usually altered the source of the problem. Organizations should therefore start their investigations into mental ill-health by examining the nature of their jobs.

Focusing upon the content of work is also valuable in enhancing the acceptability of mental health issues to managers and other employees. It is often difficult to gain company interest in the issues covered in this volume, because people prefer to give the impression that mental ill-health is a problem for someone else rather than for them. However, discussions about the effective design of jobs have clearly practical objectives, focusing upon improved work performance as well as procedures to reduce excessive employee stress.

I start from the position that some stress is inevitable in any job, as indeed in any aspect of life. That is not necessarily bad. But when job stress is extreme or extended over a long period, then we should be concerned. Our concern may be because of the harm that is being done to an employee and his or her family; or it may be because of the fact that excessive stress impairs work effectiveness, reduces productivity, and costs the organization money.

Research on the Causes of Excessive Stress at Work

Research findings in this area are based on two kinds of study. First, one can look at the people employed in different kinds of work, and ask them about their job-related anxiety, tension, distress, dissatisfaction, depression and so on, investigating how those stress reactions differ between jobs (eg Loher, Noe, Moeller, and Fitzgerald, 1985). Second, an investigator might carry out an experiment, arranging for changes to be made in a stressful job, and recording the effects of the changes in terms of employee mental health (eg Wall and Clegg, 1981). From both kinds of study, the picture is now becoming clear; there are certain features of jobs that are particularly implicated in causing excessive stress.

I will summarize those characteristics in terms of nine general features, which are present at some level in every job (Warr, 1987a). First, however, I should emphasize that at most levels those job features are not particularly problematic. Across a wide range of, say, working conditions, employees are not especially stressed. But at certain *extreme* levels, we can expect problems.

The Characteristics of Jobs which influence Stress

The nine key job characteristics can be listed as follows. In most cases, I have identified one end of the continuum for particular consideration in the present context.

1 Low job discretion

2 Low use of skills

3 Low or high work demands

4 Low task variety

5 High uncertainty

6 Low pay

7 Poor working conditions

8 Low interpersonal suport

9 Low value in society

The first feature, **low job discretion**, is particularly likely to cause excessive stress in a job. Job discretion is the most important single characteristic of work. It is absolutely essential that employees should have an area of freedom, in which they (rather than their boss or the equipment) are empowered to make decisions, to plan their work, and to tackle problems as they arise. Research has repeatedly shown that people whose jobs are excessively constraining in this respect are likely to experience undesirable levels of stress, in terms of anxiety, depression, apathy, low self-esteem and low self-confidence (eg Ganster and Fusilier, 1989).

To many readers that may sound like common sense, but in practice most organizations arrange things so that many lower-level employees have only a little opportunity to control what goes on in their work-place. People are often constrained by fixed procedures and routines, by unchangeable pacing, or by the requirements of computers or other machines.

There are a number of reasons for that, including a general wish within organizations for standardized procedures and for strong managerial control over what goes on. Yet increasing employee job discretion has the obvious benefit of permitting work problems to be tackled effectively at their source, rather than passing requests up and down a chain of command. For that pragmatic reason alone, you would expect it to be attractive to many companies.

A second feature that can give rise to excessive job stress is the **low use of skills**. It is repeatedly found that workers who have greater opportunity for skill use are mentally more healthy than colleagues with little opportunity. That relationship is found across manual jobs themselves, as well as between white- and blue-collar workers. For example, among production workers in a car factory, a particularly strong predictor of low mental health was the extent to which people felt unable to use their skills (Kornhauser, 1965).

This job characteristic is associated with the fact that employees in *lower-level* jobs are often the ones under particular stress. Research has repeatedly indicated that the poorest mental health, in terms of greater depression and lower active involvement in life, is found among workers at the bottom of an organization, not among the supposedly overstressed executives; the latter are however more likely to report job-related anxiety (eg Warr, 1990).

The harmful effect of under-use of skills means that when considering the third job feature, **work demands**, we should be concerned about very low levels as well as very high levels of demand. Particularly important are *intellectual*, as well as physical, demands. It is certain that long periods of repeated deadlines, intense concentration, and relentless pressure can cause excessive stress. There is nothing surprising about that. But it should be emphasized that very *low* work demands also impair mental health, and there are a lot of jobs that are deficient in that respect (eg Warr, 1987a).

Jobs that make very few intellectual demands on a person are also those that are low in terms of the first two features in the list: job discretion, and the use of skills. Those three features are of course overlapping in practice, and I will return to that fact later.

A fourth feature that can impair mental health is the marked absence of **task variety** in a job. Repetitive, monotonous work is soul-destroying and alienating; workers in that kind of job do not learn anything new and they have no challenges to draw them out and give them a sense of achievement. Poor mental health is common in those unchanging circumstances. That is seen both in low-level jobs and also among mid-career people at all levels who have become locked into fixed and over-familiar activities. Such people experience little active involvement in their work, and they contribute to their employer much less than they could.

A fifth potential stressor is **high uncertainty**, especially when that extends across a long period of time. There are two main forms of uncertainty at work. First is an absence of knowledge or feedback about how well you are doing, and about what kinds of behaviour are considered desirable. Second is a lack of information about the future: how likely is the company to survive, how secure is your job, or how will your career develop?

Everyone has those concerns at some time, and of course they can have an unavoidable basis in reality. Sometimes these uncertainties can be reduced, but in many cases one has to live with them. In general, however, surveys have indicated that many people believe that their employer does not take seriously enough the requirements of effective communication.

Low pay, the sixth feature, is also unavoidable in some cases. Nevertheless, it is undoubtedly true that people living in very difficult financial circumstances exhibit considerable mental ill-health of the kind discussed here. As a major job stressor, I take it that we should concentrate on those low levels of income that are clearly harmful. People will always grumble about their pay and its comparability with others, and I certainly would not count those quite normal grumbles as evidence of excessive stress.

Seventh in the list are **poor working conditions**. In a sense, several of the previous features represent poor conditions of a psychological and social kind; the focus in item seven is on poor *physical* conditions. Particularly noisy, hot, wet, or dangerous environments, from which a person cannot escape, are known to be associated with employee stress. Of course, poor physical conditions in a job are often accompanied by other stressful features of the kind I have already mentioned.

Low interpersonal support at work has been found to be associated with high anxiety, emotional exhaustion, job tension, and low job and life satisfaction. I would emphasize again that it is only when support is extremely low that we are justified in seeing that as a cause of excessive job stress.

Finally, research has pointed to the negative impact of being employed in a job which is viewed as being of **low value in society**. People see their jobs as important or unimportant to them in various ways, one of which is their contribution to society. Many jobs, in medicine for instance, can be very satisfying in those terms. Most other jobs are broadly neutral in this respect, but some are clearly viewed as 'the dregs'. Given that such low-value work has to be done by someone, it is not clear how that evaluation can be changed, and I include this theme mainly for completeness.

The Distribution of these Job Characteristics

What can be said about the pattern of these nine job features in work as a whole? It seems to be the case that *lower level positions* in British industry and commerce are constrained in such a way that often there are only low levels of the first four features. Of course, that does not necessarily lead to mental ill-health, but it certainly makes it more likely in the extreme cases I have been considering. For *managers*, high work demands and high uncertainty (features 3 and 5) are perhaps more prevalent, so that their stresses (if any) are likely to have a different source.

In many cases, it is the *combination* of job features that we need to consider. For instance, very low use of skills is in practice likely to be accompanied by low job discretion. However, less obvious combinations may arise from seemingly sound management motives. In one company that was introducing new computer-based equipment, operators were now required to attend very closely to their equipment for long periods. The job was altered in ways which demanded careful and continuous monitoring. Those greater attentional demands increased operator stress levels, but arguably to a still acceptable level.

However, the company thought it appropriate to transfer to the new machines their most expensive products, so that the employees were now responsible for material that was worth many thousand pounds. That material could be lost by a mistake on their part; and the additional cost responsibility *in conjunction with* the raised attentional demands proved to be particularly stressful (Martin and Wall, 1989). Such a high level of stress could quite easily have been avoided, by rescheduling the work, but of course the problem had to be recognized in the first place.

One combination that is especially harmful is found in jobs that have both very high work demands and very low employee discretion. Many investigations have shown that this particular combination (high demands and low discretion) gives rise to lowered mental health and a range of physical symptoms, including an increased risk of heart attacks and other cardiac problems (eg Karasek and Theorell, 1990). If the *combination* of the two potential stressors can be avoided, then high work demands can often be handled well. Hard work alone is not necessarily an excessive stressor, but sustained hard work in the absence of personal discretion is definitely harmful.

That leads on to the general, over-riding, importance of employee job discretion. An absence of the opportunity to make decisions about how to get the work done is the primary source of unacceptable stress. From a lack of discretion flow the restricted use of skills, low job variety, and other problems within the nine features I have listed previously. Conversely, if a job is designed to permit employees to control some important aspects of their work, it will be necessary for them to possess and use relevant skills, and they will have the ability to introduce some variation into what they do. In addition, raised job discretion allows people to tackle unavoidable demands at times and in ways that are most satisfactory to them.

How may Unacceptable Job Stress be Reduced?

It follows from the section above that the primary way to reduce unacceptable job stress is to enhance employee job discretion. However, there are several other actions that need to be considered. I think that there are four main steps in redesigning jobs.

First, it is obvious that we have to think seriously about possible sources of stress: which job features in our organization are likely to be particularly harmful? We should review work in terms of the nine characteristics I have described, and particularly look out for combinations of those features which might be *unexpectedly* stressful.

Assuming that we identify some jobs that appear to be problematic, we have to be realistic. The second step is to decide what can, and what cannot, be changed. In some cases, there is not much that can be done without enormous expenditure. In those cases, the situation will probably have to remain as it is, but we can achieve a lot by rotating people between roles, so that any one worker is not exposed to the same stressors continuously and for long periods.

Third, we must try to tackle isolated problems one by one. For instance, if our enquiries reveal that the level of experienced uncertainty is so great that action is warranted, we might develop and implement new communication and feedback procedures. Or it might be possible and desirable to change some aspects of the physical working conditions.

The fourth step is the one with widest applicability and importance. Management should recognize the value of introducing into jobs greater freedom of action by lower-level employees. For the reasons I have outlined, that one step can have the greatest impact on excessively high levels of stress.

The downwards delegation of decision-making can also be very effective in increasing productivity. When employees are required, and trusted, to understand how their equipment functions, to think ahead to anticipate problems, and to take action to meet current targets, then their performance will be better than if they merely respond retrospectively to problems by calling on someone else to sort out the difficulty.

One important research finding is that the productivity benefits of downwards delegation are especially great in relatively unpredictable situations, when machine errors are likely to occur, or when materials are especially variable (Wall, Corbett, Martin, Clegg, and Jackson, 1990). That is especially notable, since in those unpredictable settings management is liable to move in the opposite direction – centralizing rather than devolving the authority for action.

Conclusions

Many British companies are now moving towards greater discretion for lower-level employees, and it has been commonplace for a long time in some other countries. In practice, the downward delegation of decision-making often creates the need for increased training, so that people can acquire the required knowledge and skills. It may also be helpful to permit *groups* of workers to decide among themselves how things should be done. That in turn requires more flexibility of procedures so that people can undertake a range of different activities.

Trade unions have often resisted developments of that kind, although they are increasingly seeing their value, especially when increased responsibility is accompanied by increased wages. However, greater discretion for low-level workers means that the jobs of chargehands or supervisors may need to be changed; there can be resistance from that quarter. Associated with that is the fact that financial savings can flow from a reduced need for supervisory staff, to counterbalance the increased responsibility and pay for lower-level employees.

Although I am recommending increased job discretion as a general approach to the reduction of excessive stress, it is clear that changes of that kind can themselves initially generate *more* stress. In terms of the job features I described previously, the new stress is mainly in terms of increased uncertainty: people initially have inadequate skills and knowledge, they do not know what to do, there may be conflicts between groups, and the future is unclear.

There is thus a paradox. In order to reduce the excessive stress arising from low discretion, low skill use and low work demands, it is often necessary to move through a period of enhanced stress, albeit of a different kind. Employees have to live with increased uncertainty, initially at a high level. For that period of change there is a need for careful planning, increased training and support for people to learn new things, and a willingness to amend decisions if they do not work out well. In a sense, then, we may sometimes have to make matters worse before they become better.

However, the important point here is that the *interim* stresses which are increased in a programme of downward delegation have the potential for developing employee skills and increasing personal competence, self-confidence, and job involvement. If the necessary changes can be worked through, both employees and the organization can become more confident and more effective.

The focus of this book is in terms of excessive stress and improved mental health, and positive changes in those terms are of course inherently desirable. But, in addition to that inherent value, I am forcefully struck by the findings from research of several kinds, that excessive stress is bad for business. Managers are sometimes unimpressed by recommendations about stress-reduction, partly because it is not always clear when normal stress reaches a level that is unacceptable. However, procedures to manage stress are often the same as those which increase productivity. In many organizations, the procedures I have outlined can pay off in both respects: reducing stress and also increasing productivity.

Further Reading

Broad-ranging discussions of important job features are presented by Karasek and Theorell (1990) and Warr (1987a). Briefer accounts are in the book edited by Warr (1987b). Issues of employee job discretion are examined in depth by authors in Sauter, Hurrell, and Cooper (1989).

A comprehensive discussion of procedures and problems in modifying jobs and organizations is provided by Lawler (1986).

References

Firth, J. and Shapiro, D. A. (1986). An evaluation of psychotherapy for job-related distress. *Journal of Occupational Psychology*, **59**, 111–119.

Ganster, D. C. and Fusilier, M. R. (1989). Control in the workplace. In C. L. Cooper and I. Robertson (eds.), *International Review of Industrial and Organizational Psychology* (pp. 235–280). Chichester: Wiley.

Karasek, R. and Theorell, T. (1990). *Healthy Work: Stress, Productivity, and the Reconstruction of Working Life*. New York: Basic Books.

Kornhauser, A. W. (1965). *Mental Health of the Industrial Worker*. New York: Wiley.

Lawler, E. E. (1986). *High-involvement Management*. San Francisco: Jossey-Bass.

Loher, B. T., Noe, R. A., Moeller, N. L., and Fitzgerald, M. P. (1985). A meta-analysis of the relation of job characteristics to job satisfaction. *Journal of Applied Psychology*, **70**, 280–289.

Martin, R. and Wall, T. D. (1989). Attentional demand and cost responsibility as stressors in shop-floor jobs. *Academy of Management Journal*. **32**, 69–86.

Sauter, S. L., Hurrell, J. J., and Cooper, C. L. (eds.) (1989). *Job Control and Worker Health*. Chichester: Wiley.

Wall, T. D. and Clegg, C. W. (1981). A longitudinal field study of group work design. *Journal of Occupational Behaviour*, **2**, 31–49.

Wall, T. D., Corbett, J. M., Martin, R., Clegg, C. W., and Jackson, P. R. (1990). Advanced manufacturing technology, work design, and performance: A change study. *Journal of Applied Psychology*, **75**, 691-697.

Warr, P. B. (1987a). *Work, Unemployment, and Mental Health*. Oxford: Oxford University Press.

Warr, P. B. (ed.) (1987b). *Psychology at Work* (third edition). Harmondsworth: Penguin.

Warr, P. B. (1990). The measurement of well-being and other aspects of mental health. *Journal of Occupational Psychology*, **63**, 193–210.

5

COUNSELLING – ITS VALUE TO THE BUSINESS

Michael Reddy

Introduction

A paper with this title would have been unthinkable a couple of years or so ago. Until recently employers have remained largely unaware of counselling and not much help had been given Chief Executives to trace the straightline equation between counselling and running a profitable business.

Research

Nor, of course, to go one stage further back, have we in Britain sought to quantify what stress is costing UK business in more than global terms – in the sort of astronomical figures which leave one too daunted to even contemplate remedial action. The Americans embarked on more fine-grained research 30 years ago, starting with detailed calculations of the burden which alcohol and drug abuse alone were putting on the US economy. This showed where the damage was occurring at grassroots level and where the leverage to change things could be found.

Since then the scope of this research has been widened to include all aspects of stress. There are now hundreds of reports linking the consequent introduction of health education and counselling services with quite substantial gains in figures for absenteeism, unwanted staff departures, industrial accidents, medical and related insurance costs, and so on.

One such report, from a railroad company, illustrates the typical trend in performance indicators from employees who have used the company-sponsored counselling service. (See Table 1)

Employee assistance programmes

Most of these counselling services have for historical reasons acquired the generic title of Employee Assistance Programmes

TABLE 1   *Job Performance Changes following use of counselling service*

Indicators (Previous Month)	When first seen	At 3 Month Follow-Up	At 12 Month Follow-Up
Used health insurance	17%	8%	5%
Arrived late for work	17%	5%	3%
Left work early	13%	4%	3%
Took sick days	18%	7%	8%
Used medical leave	4%	7%	4%
Job in jeopardy	25%	7%	4%

Reproduced by permission from Spicer, J. (1987). The EAP Solution, Current Trends and Future Issues, Hazelden Foundation, Centre City, MN.

(EAP). Essentially they consist of a 24-hour telephone helpdesk and access to a national network of counsellors. Such networks already exist in the UK and are increasingly used by employers as a built-in shock absorber to the effects of stress.

What are these counsellors dealing with?

Where the service is 'broadbrush' rather than with a uniquely alcohol and drug focus, the most common categories of problem area are debt, health, marriage, general emotional disturbance, and especially anxiety. Alcohol and drug dependency accounts for only about 10% of presenting problems (though the proportion rises when underlying issues are also assessed). General personal distress plus marriage or family conflict account for well over half of the counsellor's daily task. Job pressures are the primary source of stress in 30% of cases, and are implicated in another 30%.

Only a tiny proportion of those who use counselling services would be diagnosed as mentally ill in any shape or form. What most counsellors are dealing with are 'excesses' in one of a number of key areas. In one or the other – often in two or three at the same time – people have overspent their 'capital', their credit, their resources and are, so to speak, temporarily running in the red.

This is most obvious in the case of financial resources. Government agencies, in-company and external advisers are overrun at the present moment with the all-pervasive need for debt counselling. It is, however, just as tempting for many to 'overspend' in other areas:

physical resources

social resources

psychological resources

skills resources

Stress

In a variety of ways people run down their 'current account' in these four areas by

1 being too prodigal or complacent with health (taking chances, taking too little care);

2 neglecting social networks, affectionate relationships in favour of the demands of work;

3 putting in jeopardy decisions and that all-important intuition for risk, challenge and self-belief through over-immersion in work;

4 living on the edge of their skills repertoire and experience in relation to the work they have to do.

Stress is about living beyond one's means. It is not the same as pressure. There are people in every organisation who make a virtue out of the pressure they are under. I can accept that. On balance, pressure is needed to improve performance. But that isn't what stress is about. Stress describes the unwanted effects of *too much* pressure – or sometimes, too little. In most cases it comes from too much pressure.

Stress management

To what extent all this is the inevitable cost of the way many of us live our lives and of the tremendous commercial pressures of a recessionary world economy we may leave to another volume. The medicine which governments are prescribing mean that businesses which survive are learning new habits. It is common-place to see the recession of the 90s as the price of squeezing debt out of the over-heated economy of the 80's, both corporate and personal. We are learning all over again to live within our means.

Stress management is essentially about the same thing – helping both individuals and organisations to boost their resources – whether it be financial, physical, social, psychological resources or job skills – and to live within them as much as possible. Stress management is a handy idiom to describe this process.

It is a process which counsellors take people through every day. The approach is impartial, confidential and pragmatic, while remaining sympathetic, and offers people the space to sort out priorities, feelings, goals, ideas and options, while tapping into the counsellor's own considerable experience. This will include a wealth of information about alternative sources of solution and help and, with the larger counselling firms, access to a range of computerised databases.

Changing attitudes among employers

From recent discussions with over a hundred UK companies I know that much of the above is familiar to many employers. A sea-change in attitude gathered pace during 1991. Counselling itself seems suddenly to have come of age and to have learned to demonstrate its value in commercial terms.

Meanwhile, through their closer acquaintance, sometimes at second hand, sometimes even at first, with various forms of help – debt counselling, marital counselling, crisis counselling and so on – many senior managers now well understand counselling for precisely what it is: practical, problem-solving, focused and essentially short-term assistance. Counselling enables people (sometimes in a single session) to rediscover their constructive energies and mobilise for action.

Employers are thus more and more aware that counselling is an inexpensive tool – and a cost-effective one.

They are aware furthermore that – far from being for wimps and wallies – the payoff from counselling is at its greatest where key individuals are concerned, for that core of people, precious to every employer, who add value to the business far in excess of what they take out. Some of them do so, of course, at the expense of other areas of their lives.

Many of the people I see these days fall into this category – the technical expert, the functional specialist, the senior manager under exceptional pressure, occasionally in real crisis.

These are the sort of people who easily fall into the trap of running down their resources (health, financial, social, psychological) in the way I have just described. To provide the opportunity for counselling is seen by some employers as one very practical thing they can offer in return. The fact that it also makes good commercial sense is a double bonus.

Thus counselling has taken its place over the last two or three years among a range of measures for maintaining the performance and commitment as well as the mental health of the workforce.

Current organisational climate

The reason why this has happened so relatively quickly is that the implications of counselling for the company as a whole can and should be set against a wider backcloth than simply that of individual employees.

A discussion with two Board members of a flagship UK company sticks in my mind. They were exploring the benefits of employee counselling in the context of an industry under mounting pressure. 'This won't give them the impression we care from them as individuals, will it?' asked one awkwardly. 'Mustn't raise expectations . . .' said the other. And there the matter rested. The fact that the company's shares have been on the slide ever since must just be a coincidence.

This exchange is illustrative of the way in which provision of counselling services carries overtones of company policy and attitudes in a more significant way than may be immediately apparent. Indeed there are a number of factors in the current climate which have influenced decision-makers to take a long hard look at counselling, even aside from the fact that it is a quite inexpensive employee benefit and one which is likely to pay for itself in cash terms.

Customer care

The now prevalent marketing culture throughout business has generated a range of customer care programmes and 'charters' which have inevitably broadened into a recognition of employees as internal customers to each other; and thus into staff charters and into new realms of staff care and benefits. Counselling is a welcome addition to what can be offered.

Reductions in welfare provision
A number of organisations with a strong welfare tradition are seeing such provision as in need of renewal (if they keep it at all) and related to a more paternalist culture from which they want to distance themselves.

Health initiatives
As well as being a convenient shorthand for the unwanted consequences of too much pressure, stress is also a useful portfolio term for the considerable area of overlap between physical and psychological distress. After hairdressers and bar-tenders no one hears more about personal problems than nurses and doctors. In organisations which have an occupational health unit it is usually the Chief Medical Officer or the Occupational Health Nurse who is best placed to document the rising cost of sickness and absence, and to confirm that the majority of physical ailments are overlaid with the need for counselling as much as for medicine.

Counselling as a profession
Meantime counselling has emerged as a profession, quite separate from any other – psychology, medicine, social work – with its own disciplines, codes of practice and systems of accreditation. Its approach is relatively streamlined, its methods have been well tested, its philosophy is rooted in learning theory rather than in the medical model, which means in turn that people are expected to take major responsibility for solving their own problems.

Changes in personnel strategies
The emergence of a new discipline of counselling has coincided with a shift of emphasis within the personnel profession towards a more proactive human resource development role and away from 'fixing' anything that happens to do with people. Some personnel specialists have over the years become extremely proficient and sensitive counsellors but still expect

managers and supervisors to play their part as first line 'counsellors'.

Line management responsibilities

Line managers are increasingly expected to accept the prime responsibility for the general well-being of employees. What is bothering an individual employee may sometimes relate directly and uniquely to the work situation, but as likely as not it encroaches on private, social and domestic matters. Many line managers will have neither the talent nor the stomach for such things.

They may expecially not have the *time*. One of the commonest reactions to counselling services where they have been introduced has been the enthusiastic welcome from managers, including those initially sceptical, in terms of management time that has been saved.

Management development

This enthusiastic response from line managers has often led naturally to requests to help them better understand the nature of counselling and of its boundaries with their own legitimate concerns. This process in itself frequently offers illuminating insight into the nature of the management task.

The only real resistance to counselling indeed comes from those industries or organisations (often family firms, often with their roots in previous centuries) where the culture is one of 'looking after our people' and where a counselling service could be seen as an invasion of the special relationship between manager and employee.

There is a second, related, fear among some managers that a counselling service would cut them off from a lot of information they are entitled to on a 'need to know' basis. The fact of course is that most of what counsellors hear is precisely what the employee would not breathe within the organisation's four walls at any price.

In any case, to the extent that such concern is realistic, there are a number of mechanisms for making sure that the organisation's needs are not neglected in the process of protecting individual confidentiality. Counselling services should provide both statistical and qualitative data on levels and themes of uptake if only to meet the requirement of adequate accountability. My own experience is one of needing close working relationships with the organisation at all levels simply to put more value into the counselling itself. Counselling service providers should not be allowed to operate too much at arm's length.

Contracting out
At the same time, in the context of evolving organisational structures, counselling services are a natural candidate for contracting out. For most organisations under two or three thousand strong they are difficult to operate economically at necessary levels of professionalism.

Counselling skills training
Counselling services often lead more broadly to the introduction of counselling skills training for a cross section of staff throughout the organisation – supervisors, personnel, welfare, occupational health and training officers, for example, with the emphasis sometimes on general techniques of counselling, sometimes focusing on specific areas such as bereavement, customer violence, trauma counselling, alcohol, drugs and so on.

Organisation Development
More significant still has been the importation of counselling – both its techniques and its philosophy – into organisational processes such as appraisal, day-to-day performance management, assessment and development centres and career management. I remember a Board meeting where the concept of counselling was introduced in the context of career management: 'If we could put something like this in place", said one member, 'the company would change out of all recognition'.

Change Management
It falls to me regularly to alert senior management to the far-reaching effects which counselling can have on the way an entire company goes about its business. As is demonstrated in one of the examples above, some cultures simply aren't ready for it. On the other hand, there are companies which have

adopted counselling – again, both its techniques and its philosophy – precisely to announce a change in culture and to act as its vehicle.

One such organisation (it describes itself as 'macho' but then which organisation doesn't?) has had a counselling service for four years now and has recently expanded it to include spouses. One of its employees who had suffered an unusually unpleasant experience was publicly very positive about the help he had received from counselling and gave the service credit for the fact that he had not missed a day's work. 'If you need counselling', said his immediate boss, 'then I don't need you!' Four years ago that would have been the end of the matter, but not any more. This time the deputy CEO moved quickly to reprimand the supervisor in no uncertain terms for his 'caveman' attitude – an interesting switch in vocabulary.

Conclusion

I have attempted to relate the still largely unexploited benefits of counselling to the management of stress, and in the context of organisational change.

The value of counselling to individuals is self-evident and nothing beyond the obvious has been said here. What may have been less obvious is that stress in an organisation is not an individual phenomenon. Stress management relates only partly to the stressproofing of individuals. Stress can as easily arise out of a whole range of dissonances at the heart of organisational policies, procedures and structures. In this respect I have sought to demonstrate the potential contribution of counselling at the macro as well as the micro level.

References

Edwards, H. *Psychological Problems – Who Can Help?*, 1987 The British Psychological Society.

Hoskinson, L. *Counselling in UK Organisations* ICAS 1989, PO Box 615, Aspley Guise, Milton Keynes MK17 8DB.

Reddy, M. *The Manager's Guide to Counselling at Work*, 1987, Routledge.

Spicer, J. *The EAP Solution*, 1987, Hazelden.

6

WORK PROBLEMS CAUSED BY MENTAL ILL HEALTH AND THEIR MANAGEMENT

Doreen Miller

Introduction

Marks and Spencer is an international retailer with 291 stores employing 60,000 people of whom 83% are female and 62% part time. Our working population in stores and warehouses is a tightly knit community consisting of members of commercial, personnel and administrative management, and sales and warehouse staff. Teamwork is important in every job and good two way communication is essential at all levels. Every store has a communication group chaired by an elected member of staff. Our business momentum week by week is driven by the previous week's sales figures and the staff morale reflects these takings in every part of the company.

Recent organisational changes

During the last 7–8 years there has been a lot of change in the business:

- In 1983 Lord Rayner was the first non-family member to become Chairman.

- In the last 5–6 years following the appointment of a new Finance Director, the Company experienced a new style of financial management, with greater accountability in every department in the business. Even Health Services became involved in submitting an annual financial operating plan.

- New computer systems emerged to record sales, order stock from suppliers, and streamline deliveries to stores.

- During the last few years a new system of job evaluation has been introduced with a new form of appraisal and reward package.

- Earlier this year, following a Head Office restructure, 300 people were made redundant and a further number took advantage of the voluntary redundancy package. This was an event not previously experienced by present employees and one which affected all those who remained as well as those who left.

Marks and Spencer is not alone in experiencing these changes. Many other large companies have been similarly affected with dramatic effects arising from restructuring, delayering and downsizing.

The effect of information technology cannot be overlooked. People are faced with more information being available on the screen leading to quicker decision making compared with gathering information from paper sources. Work at visual display terminals may lead to social isolation of staff creating different needs at breaks and different patterns of work. Fatigue too may affect those involved in screen based work unless the job design is carefully considered.

A lot of change – for some too much too quickly. Many people can cope, but some fail when this degree of change occurs at work combined with other changes in their lives outside. Pressures ensue which may ultimately lead to mental ill health.

Work problems caused by mental ill health

What are the problems at work caused by mental ill health and how are they managed? The mental health conditions that one commonly sees at work are anxiety and/or depression. The presenting problems may be as follows:

* The person may come to work but their performance is noticeably affected and productivity reduced.

* Errors may start to appear in their work, or poor inter-personnel relationships arise with colleagues or customers.

* Low morale of a team may be the presenting symptom arising from an individual team member's persistent poor performance or absence associated with anxiety or depression.

* Accidents at work may be another presenting problem

* Ultimately, persistent symptoms, or repeated absence arising from symptoms may lead to permanent withdrawal
  from work.

* Labour turnover, absence and accidents are costly events
  whatever the cause.

The role of the Occupational Health Service

In our Occupational Health Service we work closely with personnel and line management to look after the investment in our staff
– our most valuable resource. Our responsibility is to ensure that
we select people who are suitable for the work and maintain
them in the best state of mental, physical and social well being. In
so doing, we aim to get the best productivity from our staff.

We have a team of doctors, dentists, oral hygienists, nurses and
physiotherapists in our Head Office. All stores have a visiting
doctor, chriopodist and dentist and 20 of our largest stores have a
full time nurse.

The occupational health team is available to look at the effects of
health on work, or work on health, to discuss with staff any
health problems they may have, and to promote good health
through health education, screening, and action programmes.

(a) Assessment of the context of the health problem

The context may be social, physical or environmental. It may be
the current socio-economic climate in the country such as the
present state of recession with attendant unemployment of
partners in a predominantly female workforce. In some parts of
the country where there is high unemployment our staff have
become the 'breadwinners' of the family. It may be the management policies in the company or department. It may be the
physical working environment – heating, lighting, ventilation,
noise levels. It may be the family in which relationships may be
supportive or not. One's religion, too, may play a part when it
contributes to feelings, attitudes, lifestyle and the social support
system in life.

(b) Assessment of vulnerability

If the 'context' covers aspects of the external environment
'vulnerability' refers to the internal environment, the 'you and
me' factors which are probably of greater importance.

An individual's personality traits influence his vulnerability, although they may be modified by training and experience as time goes by.

Peaks of concern leading to vulnerability may arise at the time of the first job, leaving school and sometimes home. The time of marriage, of maternity leave, with the question about return to work thereafter, mid-career review or pre-retirement concerns about 'what next' may all contribute to vulnerability. In all instances, where there is more knowledge about the subject concerned so the anxiety and vulnerability is reduced.

As in other companies, we are now planning pre-retirement courses at a younger age – at 50 instead of 55 – and now financial planning courses are held for staff in their 40's to enable people to plan ahead and reduce anxieties when the time of retirement comes.

People may find that they are more vulnerable if they take a job which is not suited to their intellect. The highly educated or highly intelligent individual may have problems in performing an unskilled job which he/she has taken for monetary gain; the converse is equally true.

Physical health is important as physical illness may increase emotional vulnerability as well as result from it.

(c) Assessment of the immediate stressors

Stressors at home may arise from pressures associated with the spouse, children or care needs of an elderly relative or financial problems.

One of the greatest pressures leading to mental ill health is *unemployment* when feelings of lack of belonging, worthlessness and lack of daily routine prevail. However those in employment may also feel vulnerable. Job responsibilities, if unclear, may lead to uncertainty and anxiety about ones value and a feeling of reduced job satisfaction.

Too much work may lead to anxiety, particularly if the responsibilities are unfamiliar to the person. The good technologist may become ineffective as a technical manager if he has limited managerial skills.

Work underload leads to doubts about one's value, worth and self esteem and anxiety may follow although, following restructuring, this is not a common problem in Marks and Spencer at present.

Role ambiguity and conflict may occur in taking on new responsibilities or in dual career families. Often the working mother who is responsible for the home family and her career may be particularly affected.

Travel may create anxiety particularly if the journey is complex. The long comfortable intercity journey may be more relaxing than the commuter journey involving several changes of vehicle.

Communications at work should be the correct communication to the right people at the right time and preferably two ways.

Many of the pressures mentioned relate to change and if there are *too many changes too quickly*, when a person is vulnerable for one reason or another, without a supportive climate, symptoms of mental ill health may arise. The occupational health service members ensure that they are commercially aware of new developments in the business, new equipment, new systems of work and new work practices. Good working relationships between the Occupational Health Service and management is vital.

(d) Assessment of symptoms

The nurse/doctor needs to have time to listen. Often when discussing a physical symptom, eg headache, indigestion, backache, the clue to the underlying anxiety or depression emerges.

The problems may often be multiple, eg unemployment, financial difficulties, school children, and elderly relatives. The 'final straw' to trigger the anxiety at work may be quite a minor incident such as a 'ticking off' from a supervisor or a task not completed on time.

(e) Management of symptoms

Following discussion about a health symptom and the underlying cause, having 'dumped the problem', the member of staff will return to work less anxious, and more productive. At times action may be needed by the members of the Occupational

Health Service to refer a member of staff to the General Practitioner, a psychologist or psychiatrist.

We work closely with General Practitioners to take action in reviewing the work and out of work picture of a problem. Sometimes dramatic results can be achieved by 2 or 3 visits to a psychologist to provide coping strategies.

Sadly in some parts of the country there are long waiting lists to see psychologists in the NHS which in turn prolongs the state of anxiety/depression and the absence from work. In addition, some Private Health Insurance Companies fail to provide cover for mental ill health. We have negotiated with our insurer to provide cover for in-patient and out-patient psychiatric services including psychologists. Our Occupational Health Service negotiates annual premiums directly with the Private Health Insurance company and employees pay their own premiums in the company scheme.

We often find that by working with GP, psychiatrist, psychologist we can modify the work pattern and responsibilities to enable the person to stay at work and feel that he is contributing in a positive way rather than fostering feelings of worthlessness and low morale by prolonging absence.

(f) Liaison with management

The organisation can assist in preventing mental ill health by giving people a good working environment and a clearly defined job. Following absence it is often essential to be able to modify the working hours during the rehabilitation period to provide a gradual return to usual working practices through a good sick pay scheme. Financial support at this time will allay anxiety and encourage a speedier return to work.

Regular honest appraisals are important and problems in performance should be discussed at the time of occurrence, with an opportunity to follow up and review progress. People should feel able to contribute to their own development and feel accountable for the job.

Where counselling facilities from personnel or health professionals are available time away from work is saved.

The health of the nation

The Health of the Nation discussion document sets out the government proposals for the development of a health strategy for England. It mentions the role of the employers in the promotion of people's health. This is appropriate for people spending a large amount of their lives at work. No one health professional or employer holds the monopoly on health promotion. It is everyone's business. We believe that the Occupational Health Service through Health Promotion can assist employees in acquiring more knowledge on health topics. For where there is knowledge there is understanding.

Marks and Spencer's strategy for health promotion

Our strategy for health promotion at Marks and Spencer is based on:

- Health education to raise awareness of factors affecting health and wellbeing.

- Screening programmes to detect risk factors or early signs of disease.

- Action programmes to do something about them.

We aim to provide health education programmes based on guided self help and our team works with the Health Education Council. During the last 5 years exhibition material on stress, diet, exercise, smoking and alcohol has toured all stores. We are planning new programmes on osteoporosis and Aids.

We use videos for our screening programmes including a video on testicular cancer. The videos may be taken home by staff, thus providing the whole family with the opportunity for further information.

Our action programmes relate to chiropody, physiotherapy treatment, referral to a consultant for further advice. Fitness programmes or relaxation techniques are being developed at present.

Conclusions

We believe that an Occupational Health Service can play a major part in helping

- to identify work problems caused by mental ill health

- to take action to improve the health of employees

- to assist employers in modifying the work and work environment

- to enable employees to remain at work rather than withdraw.

In so doing we can optimise the productivity of people at work and achieve a high quality of service to the customer.

7

COUNSELLING IN THE POST OFFICE

Richard Welch and Noreen Tehrani

Introduction

The Post Office, as one of the largest employers in the UK, has always taken its responsibility towards its workforce seriously. This caring approach goes back a long time, with a Welfare service and an Occupational Health Service (OHS), each with nationwide responsibility. In the early 1980s, well before the advent of the Employee Assistance Programmes in Britain, it had become clear to senior management in Occupational Health that there was a need to provide some form of emotional and psychological support to employees. It was felt that this support could best be provided by an internal counselling service.

The Counselling Pilot study, which came out of the recommendations of an OHS working party was the first of its kind in the UK and was able to demonstrate that there were definite cost and organisational benefits from the introduction of a counselling service into the business. In addition to providing a specialist counselling resource, in the form of two specialist counsellors, there were also significant benefits obtained from two additional initiatives. Firstly the introduction of a training programme for Occupational Health Professionals which enhanced first line counselling skills and secondly the development of a Stress Education Seminar Programme which trained the Occupational health Doctors and Nurses to educate line managers in the identification of stress symptoms, outlined the reasons why stress occurs both at home and in the workplace and encouraged the development of skills which could be used to alleviate stress symptoms.

The pilot study was completed in 1990 and the process of evaluating the findings in relationship to the constantly changing needs of a dynamic business and of its workforce was undertaken. The Post Office now feels that it is in a good position to move forward with the knowledge it has gained and to develop an even more appropriate, accountable and valued service for its employees.

The background to the Counselling Pilot Study

In 1984, a working party composed of Line management, Personnel and Occupational Health staff examined the need for an individual or group counselling service within the Post Office. The working party had been formed as a result of the increasing evidence which suggested that the pace of change occurring within the business at this time was leading to an increasing number of employees finding it difficult to cope. The evidence for this belief was the increased occurrence of sickness absences and of medical retirements. During this period strong competitive commercial pressures were operating on all sectors of the Post Office resulting in the need to reorganise the business into smaller business units. This led to the inevitable devolution of responsibility to lower levels of management, together with a sharper requirement for personal accountability and a progression towards a product orientated organisational structure.

The pace and size of these changes would have caused a heavy demand on any organisation, but in the Post Office, which had been traditionally slow to change and had a culture which tended to be reactive rather than innovative, these demands were all the more taxing. When external commentators suggested that the pace of change in the Post Office was in fact too slow many employees felt all the more threatened.

For many people change can represent a challenge which is necessary for their effective functioning. For organisations change may be vital for the survival and the health of the business. The level of individual and group tolerance to change may vary, but there is a certain point at which for the majority of individuals the volume of change becomes threatening and overwhelming. When individuals and groups are unable to cope with change appropriately they may develop responses to that change which are not constructive and may even be detrimental to their well-being.

Taken in a wider perspective the pressures arising from organisational change and the work situation are generally less significant than those which arise from personal problems such as family and relationship issues, housing difficulties, health concerns and financial problems. However, it is difficult to leave personal problems at home so they all may combine to bring about harmful effects at work such as lost production, lowered efficiency, increased labour turnover, impaired industrial relations and increased medical wastage.

The Working Party reported its findings in August 1985 and one of the recommendations made was to appoint two specialist counsellors for a three year pilot study based in the Manchester and Leeds areas, with control areas of equal work population size (6,000–8,000 approximately) in and around Liverpool and Newcastle upon Tyne respectively. The project was designed to assess the long term specialist counselling needs of the Post Office and was to be evaluated by the Professor of Organisational Psychology at UMIST, Prof. Cary Cooper, funded by a grant from the Health and Safety Executive.

At its inception, this project was described as 'probably one of the most exciting and ambitious projects ever undertaken by any industry in the field of occupational medicine and psycho-social research', and its findings were felt 'likely to have implications on the future of caring services at work well into the 21st century'.

The role of the Specialist Counsellors in the first half of the Pilot Study

The Specialist Counsellors were appointed as members of the professional staff of the Occupational Health Service. One Counsellor being located in the North West Area and the other in the North East Area. Each counsellor reported to the appropriate Area Medical Adviser and was appointed on a three year contract in order to:

a   Provide a specialist counselling service to the employees in their area.

b   Estimate the long term specialist counselling needs of the Post Office.

c   Identify means to reduce work-related stress.

Prior to the pilot study the established practice for Post Office employees with personal or work related problems was to contact the Occupational Health or the Welfare services to obtain advice, information and some counselling, these services often overlapping in their functions. During the pilot study the Specialist Counsellors provided an additional internal counselling service, handling the more complex and deep-seated psychological and emotional problems which would have previously been referred outside the Post Office for specialist assessment, counselling or treatment. During the pilot study access to the Specialist Counsellors was made through referrals from Occupational Health, Welfare and Personnel with the additional path of direct or open access for those employees who wished to use that route.

Typically the counselling undertaken by the Specialist Counsellors involved a series of in-depth sessions with the employee and, where necessary, relatives, with the aim of gradually bringing about changes in perspective, behaviour, self-confidence or awareness in order to assist in alleviating or overcoming the problem. This counselling process may include, for example, strengthening the employees ability to cope with a particularly stressful situation, facilitating a change of behaviour, or increasing an individual's insight to aid him or her to deal appropriately with their feelings when faced with situations or events which were outside their control.

The counselling process is often slower, less controllable and of a different nature to that of advising which means that it is not necessarily a skill which is used by the Welfare or Occupational health Advisers in the normal course of their work. In addition it would not normally be possible for Welfare or Occupational Health Advisers to give their time to counselling, as this would reduce their ability to fulfil their important primary roles.

The Specialist counsellors, as employees of the Post Office were in the privileged position of being aware of organisational changes and issues which may be influential in the employees work situation. The role also enabled them to have an opportunity to contribute to the development and implementation of company policy and procedures which could minimise or eliminate work related difficulties. These privileges gave the internal

Specialist Counsellors a distinct advantage over any external counsellor support which had previously been available.

Mid-Term Project Results

At the half way stage it was evident that there was a need for counselling and as the service became more accepted within the business the Specialist Counsellor case loads began to grow.

Many of the clients who contacted the counsellors direct did so on the recommendation of earlier satisfied clients. The results of the Pilot study were also very encouraging with the pay back to the business clearly demonstrated; principally through:

a Decrease in sickness absence, authorised special leave and disciplinary measures following counselling.

b Improved work performance as perceived by the supervisor or line manager who was aware of the counselling through the choice of the employee.

Summary of the Pilot Study at the Half Way Stage

The Chief Medical Adviser considered the findings of the first eighteen months of the project and came to the conclusion that the appointment of large numbers of specialist personal counsellors was not an economically nor organisationally viable proposition. However, it was clear that there was an employee demand and organisational need for the services of the Specialist Counsellors who were, by this stage under increasing pressure to accept cases from other Post Office areas.

It was therefore recommended that:

a The Specialist Counsellor remain as a scarce resource within the Occupational Health Service (eg one per Area).

b Each Specialist Counsellor to:

  * Be Professionally Qualified in Psychology and Counselling

  * Have at least five years post-graduate relevant counselling experience

* Be organisationally and managerially aware

* Be experienced in training professional staff

The Role of the Specialist Counsellors in the second half of the Pilot Study

Whilst the results of the first part of the pilot study had been very positive, it must be accepted that the contribution of the Specialist Counsellors to the business as a whole was limited by the smallness of the personal counselling resource they were able to offer and the relative size of the workforce (in excess of 200,000 employees). The nature of the counselling process is such that the direct contribution of the Specialist Counsellors in their personal counselling role was unlikely to be increased. It was therefore decided that the greatest payback from the appointment of the Specialist Counsellors could be obtained through the development and extension of the counselling skills of other staff, initially within the OHS. It was therefore proposed that during the second phase of the study, in addition to the personal counselling undertaken by the Specialist Counsellors, a proportion of their time should be devoted to developing and monitoring counselling skills in other professionals. It was therefore suggested that there would be three areas for action:

a Development of a fully supported Counselling Skills Programme suitable for Occupational Health Service staff initially and at a later date to be offered to Welfare and Personnel Professionals.

b Provision of adequate and appropriate supervision of staff involved in counselling.

c Development of a fully supported and widely available Stress Education package.

These duties were to be carried out in addition to the existing case work undertaken by the counsellors. It was recognised that the time available to spend on the training and development initiatives would therefore be limited.

Results at the end of the Pilot Study

The Pilot study had two major focal points in assessing the effectiveness of the counselling service provided by the Specialist

Counsellors. Firstly the effectiveness and benefits of the service from the individual clients viewpoint and secondly the benefits which accrued to the organisation. At the organisational level, objective measurement of sickness absence was used, this data being collected from the relevant employee files which are kept on a routine basis by the Post Office Personnel Department. On the individual client level, various psychological tests were used which measured such variables as well-being and attitude. The client group were matched as far as possible with an equivalent control group. In all approximately 250 clients took part in the study.

Of the clients seen by the Specialist Counsellors 49% presented problems indicating poor mental or emotional health and stress. 19% felt that their problems were due to long working hours and shift work. 18% of clients had problems with marital or other important relationships. Closer examination of the work related problems indicated that the organisational structure and climate seemed to cause the greatest difficulty, followed by conflict with the work role and with poor interpersonal relationships in the workplace.

The Individual Clients

The client group (pre counselling) seemed to be more anxious, depressed, suffered more physical complaints and had lower self esteem than their colleagues in the control group. In the organisational arena the pre counselling client group had less job satisfaction and were less committed to the organisation than the control group.

After counselling the client group showed improvement in all areas of psychological well-being together with significant changes in behaviour.

After counselling the client group had reduced their dependence on alcohol, coffee and smoking as coping mechanisms and replaced these ineffective coping behaviours with a greater use of exercise and relaxation techniques.

The Organisation

Pre counselling the client group had an average level of absence of 32.53 days in a six month period. After counselling the client group absence levels had fallen to 11.14 days against the control group with 8.82 days. Part of the fall in the absence rates of the client group may be explained by the fact that of the clients who entered counselling 22% were deemed to be unfit for work and medically retired within the course of the Pilot study. However, the reduction in sick absence is significant and has been accepted, by the Post Office, as a benefit provided by the counselling service.

Evaluation of the Cost Effectiveness of the Counselling Service

The cost effectiveness of a counselling service is very likely to be of major interest to any organisation contemplating introducing a similar service. A very crude analysis of the savings which the Specialist Counsellors were able to achieve was conducted. This analysis is difficult to quantify accurately because of the number of direct and indirect components. Direct costs to the Post Office include the wages and salaries paid during sickness absence; wages and salaries paid to employees who replace people on sick leave; recruitment and training costs paid to replace employees who take early retirement or are medically retired. There are many indirect savings which are difficult to quantify, but include increased productivity, reduction in supervisor's time dealing with problematic employees and improvements in quality of creative thinking in unstressed employees. The only element of direct savings which was calculated for the pilot study was on the wage and salary cost savings brought about by the reduction in sickness absence (this calculation does not include the costs of replacement staff employed to cover the duties of the sick employee). The cost savings evaluation took the number of sick days taken by the client in the six months pre counselling at the average daily salary level for the employee and compared that with the costs of the sick days taken during the six months following the completion of the counselling. On this basis, using the sample of 177 clients, it was estimated that there was a direct saving of around £101,993 over a six month period. As already indicated this figure does not take account of all the direct savings nor any of the indirect savings, on the other hand it also does not take account of the costs associated with setting up and running the counselling service nor the cost of the medical or early retirements.

Results of the 'Other Areas' Work

Of equal, if not greater importance to the Post Office was the development of the 'other areas' including counselling skills training for Occupational health professionals, Supervision of individuals involved in counselling and the development of the Stress Education Programme for Post Office managers. As already indicated the Specialist Counsellor's resource was stretched by the demands made on it for the provision of one to one counselling. It was possible, however to develop a comprehensive and effective counselling skills training programme for the Occupational Health Service during the latter half of the project with the majority of the Occupational Health Nurses undertaking the training.

A vital part of the Counselling Skills training involved the provision of one to one and group supervision, this facility was extended for those nurses who undertook further counselling training leading to a counselling certificate or diploma.

The Stress Education Programme, which was seen as a high priority by the organisation, was taken up by the Chief Medical Adviser who, with the assistance of outside consultants was able to develop the training for the Occupational Health team which enabled them to undertake the important and very popular Stress Education Seminars now available within the Post Office.

1. Counselling Skills Training
The rationale

Managers, supervisors, personnel and welfare officers and Occupational health specialists frequently find themselves in situations where they are required to listen and support individuals who are facing some kind of difficulty or crisis in their life. In many respects the Occupational Health nurse or doctor is in a unique position in that they are separate from the employees line management and as a feature of their professional and ethical codes of practice they are bound by very strong rules of confidentiality. These factors make the Occupational Health Service the choice route for many employees who wish to solve their personal and work related problems.

Although very important, counselling and listening skills are rarely part of the medical or occupational health training with these vital inter-personal skills often being taken for granted as they are assumed to be part of every health professional's repertoire. Even the casual observer can see that there are wide variations in individuals' abilities to listen, respond and empathise appropriately with others. For the medical professional these skills may be crucial; unless the patient feels comfortable and confident then it is unlikely that he or she will be able to disclose all the aspects of a problem and as a result may be the victim of an inappropriate diagnosis. In the words of one specialist, reported recently, 'Prothiaden (an antidepressant drug) is no substitute for this patient sorting out his marital problems'.

The course objectives

The first counselling skills course was held in 1988 and involved 10 trainees. The aims of the course were to increase the skills of the Occupational Health staff by enabling them to:

a Discuss critically a range of strategies for counselling Post Office Employees.

b Identify the limitations of counselling as a problem solving method.

c Demonstrate a range of skills in counselling.

d Use the Counselling Support Group (of colleagues undergoing training) to extend and advance their counselling skills.

e Be aware when more specialist help may be required.

The course design

Whilst constructing the course design, a balance was taken between counselling skills, knowledge and practice. The course reflected both elements with the major theoretical input being based around the book 'Counselling Skills for Nurses' by Verena Tschedin. This book was essential pre-course reading for all the trainees.

The counselling practice was designed to be as realistic as possible. This was accomplished by devoting a significant part of the course to counselling interviews. Each trainee had the opportunity to conduct two interviews each lasting for up to 45 minutes. The clients were volunteers who had previously been through a counselling experience and were able, in the view of their counsellor, to talk about their problem without any adverse reactions. This situation has an element of risk, but this was contained by ensuring that an experienced counsellor was always available should the need arise. From the trainees' point of view, providing this experience of an interview was invaluable. A video tape was taken of each counselling interview, which enabled the trainees to observe actual counselling skills in action. However helpful the two counselling interviews were, together with the observation and review of the interviews of the other trainees, it was still a restricted experience. In order to extend the practice period, it was decided to split the formal element of the training into two parts, separated by a gap of four months during which time the learning could be consolidated through using the skills with actual clients. During the consolidation period supervision and support was available from the two specialist counsellors. In addition to the support and supervision given to the trainees by the specialist counsellors, the trainees were encouraged to form support networks. This process was facilitated through group supervision during which time the group members were encouraged to present cases, resolve difficulties and seek support and help from other group members.

The Counselling Skills training programme was seen as very successful and, as a consequence, two further programmes were undertaken in 1989. These programmes built on the experience of the earlier training but in all major respects remained the same as the first course. The Post Office is aware of the multitude of Counselling Skills Training programmes which are available, but believes that this training is unique in that it has a specific focus on the needs of the Occupational Health specialist, and as such has proved to be of interest to Occupational Health Staff from other organisations who took up places on the later courses.

*Further details on the Counselling Skills Training Course can be obtained from the Occupational Health Service, Post Office, Concept 2000, 250 Farnborough Road, Farnborough, GU14 7LU.

2. Counselling Supervision

The necessity for adequate supervision of people undertaking counselling is both an ethical requirement and a recognised need for all Occupational Health Staff undertaking counselling. A number of Occupational Health Advisers (OHA) undertook additional counselling training leading to counselling diploma or certificate status. Where the OHA was in training or had completed their training in counselling, the Post Office provided one to one supervision up to British Association of Counselling standards. For OHAs who had counselling skills training telephone support was available together with the peer group support and line manager supervision from the responsible Occupational Health Physician.

3. Stress Education Seminars

It had been recognised at the half way stage of the pilot study that one of the major problems identified among employees attending the counselling sessions held by the Specialist Counsellors was stress. The Post Office had become aware in the early 1980s that psychiatric and psychological disturbances often associated with stress were the second highest reason for medical retirement, second only to musculo-skeletal problems. It seemed sensible therefore to take a pro-active stance in response to this need and to develop a programme of Stress Education Seminars. These could be held in the workplace during normal working hours and would last about 2 hours. This type of programme was much more likely to reach the attention of a wide range of the workforce than, for example, a more formal 2 day training programme on Stress Management. The major difficulty in staging the number of seminars required by the enormous workforce of the Post Office was the lack of qualified and trained presenters of the Stress Education materials. The Occupational Health Professionals were in a good position to provide the basis of the education programme with their in-depth knowledge of the physiological outcomes of excessive stress on the body. However, it was necessary to build on that knowledge the additional awareness of the psychological and emotional outcomes of stress together with a recognition of the potential stressors which commonly operate on the individual at home and in work. Finally there was a need to be able to present the material in an interesting and appropriate form which required some training in presentation techniques.

The Post Office Stress Education Package

The Occupational Health Service developed its own Stress Education Package which is made up of a presentation including overheads and presentation script, a booklet which contains useful information and two Stress questionnaires and (if required) a Relaxation Tape. A commercially available video is also used.

Stress Education Training Outline

The course introduction reviewed a physical model of stress and used this model to identify some of the areas of the Post Office where stress to employees has been noted. Some time is spent assessing the psychological aspects of stress in order that trainees would be able to identify stress symptoms in themselves and others and develop strategies to reduce stress through physical, mental and behavioural stress proofing. As the education programme was particularly concerned with the workplace as a potential stressor a significant part of the training course looked at the nature of work related stress including the personality determinants which lead to 'hurry sickness', burn out and stressful relationships. A number of stress proofing techniques were explored including Time Management, Assertiveness in the Workplace and Participation as a Management Style.

The trainees were then given a copy of the Post Office Stress Education Package with which they became familiar through review and discussion. This familiarisation preceded the introduction of the presentations skills element of the training programme. The Presentation skills training was designed to enable the Occupational Health professional to deliver the stress education packages to the employees of the Post Office. This required that the trainees became aware of the characteristics of a good presentation, understood the effect of body language and eliminated irritating verbal and physical 'habits' from their presentation. Emphasis was placed on the need to research the audience and the venue before a presentation. The trainees were also taught on the use of handouts, humour and visual aids in maximising the impact of a presentation.

The trainees were all expected to make short presentations using the Stress Education Package, each presentation was videoed so that the trainee was able to discuss performance with the other course members.

Since the introduction of the Stress Education package the Stress Seminar has become a regular event throughout the Post Office. The demand for Stress Seminars for managers and staff at all levels has not diminished over time. One of the major advantages of taking the stress seminar to the workforce is that Stress has become a more acceptable topic and therefore employees seem to be more willing to address their stress symptoms at an early stage rather than to wait until they become intractable.

Recommendations at the End of the Pilot Study

a   That confidentiality is crucial to any counsellor – client relationship and that confidentiality is only seen as certain within the Occupational Health service.

b   The Counselling service must gain acceptance within the whole of the Post Office and should involve Personnel, the Unions, Senior Management and Welfare together with Occupational Health.

c   Counsellors working within the Post Office must combine counselling with organisational skills.

d   Easy access to all employees is essential, this open access to be achieved through the self referral of employees to the Welfare and Occupational Health Service who should, where the case warranted specialist counselling, refer the employee to the specialist counsellor.

Counselling in the Post Office – Looking towards the future

The Counselling Pilot Study was completed in 1990, since which time a great deal of thought has taken place over the best way forward. Both of the original Specialist Counsellors have now left the Post Office and a single Specialist Counsellor has been appointed to take the project forward. The Post Office as a business has continued to change with greater than ever emphasis on Customer Service, Business Development, and Accountability both at a personal and financial level. The need for counselling seems to be greater than ever. The emphasis now is even more than before on value for money, accountability and cost benefit analysis. It is incumbent on the new Specialist Counsellor together with the Occupational Health Service to provide the direction and momentum to a more effective and appropriate counselling service than was provided by the pilot study.

In response to this objective a new counselling strategy is being developed. The main features of the strategy include:

a   The development of a recognised counselling skills training course which would be appropriate for training pro-fessionals from all of the Post Office's employee support services and line management.

b   Training for all people using counselling and counselling skills in assessment of counselling needs and making appropriate and timely referrals.

c   The establishment of agreed and measurable counselling objectives to be used to monitor the effectiveness of the counselling service.

d   Clarification of the roles of the support services and increased co-operation between the services to benefit the employee.

e   Increased awareness of the needs of the business in order to provide the necessary support in the development of procedures and policy which take account of the employee's physical, emotional and psychological well being.

f   Development of further educational packages aimed at improving the employee's emotional and psychological health through greater awareness of potential and actual personal or work related problems.

g   Ensure that all counselling and counselling skills work is undertaken in an environment which is ethical and secure for both the client and the counsellor.

h   Develop a network of external counsellors and specialists who are competent and appropriate to the work that they undertake on behalf of the Post Office.

Conclusions

The Post Office is confident that its latest strategy on employee counselling is one which will work. The use of existing tried and tested first line counselling skills available in Occupational Health, Welfare and Personnel Services forms a solid base on which the counselling service can grow.

The additional training and supervision of the front line counselling skills professionals will ensure that the quality of the service is enhanced through appropriate information, advice and referral where necessary.

The development of an external network of qualified and experienced counsellors increases the flexibility of the counselling approach and is much more cost effective than having in-house Specialist Counsellors who are unable to specialise in more than one or two counselling areas.

At a time when monitoring the cost effectiveness of all services is paramount to business, counselling must be able to show that it provides a tangible benefit to the organisation in terms of improved productivity leading to enhanced profitability, the plans to include monitoring in terms of hard and soft data form part of the current strategy to give the customer, in the form of the organisation and the employee, what they want.

Finally the pro-active approach of taking counselling to the employee through the development of the eduational seminar or workshop increases the effectiveness of the service by enhancing awareness of potential problems. This enables the Post Office Counselling Service to provide the best possible service for all its customers.

8

Managing Mental Health Problems for a Large Workforce*

*D. K. Nichol and A. D. Bacon***

Introduction

Quite apart from a desire to help prevent suffering and misery, those responsible for managing the National Health Service have two very tangible reasons for being concerned about the mental health of its workforce. First, there is the loss of output due to staff absence and under-performance. Second, treating staff for preventable mental health problems consumes resources that would otherwise be available for other forms of health care.

Loss of output

The total loss in output is a combination of the following:

a certificated absence from work where the reason given on the certificate involves some form of mental health problem such as depression or nervous exhaustion;

b certificated absence from work where the reason given on the certificate is not explicitly mental health related, but where it is the individual's current mental health state that accounts for his or her need to be off work[1];

c uncertificated absence – the first five days absence by full time employees and absence by part time employees where the cause is primarily one of mental ill health;

d under-performance by staff who remain at work but whose capacity to work normally is impaired by mental health problems.

---

*   This is an expanded version of the paper given by Mr Nichol at the CBI Conference on 13 November 1991.

**   Mr Nichol is Chief Executive of the National Health Service. Mr Bacon heads the Chief Executive's Policy Unit.

There seem to be no NHS-wide, research based figures for any of these, and for some even making reasonable estimates would be very difficult. But there can be no real doubt that the total loss of output is very great. For example, studies suggest that health service workers are at least as likely as employees generally to suffer from mental health problems[2]. Applying the national rate of absence from work where the reason given on the certificate involves some form of mental health problem to the number of full time NHS employees, (nearly 600,000 in England), suggests that every year the NHS loses output equivalent to the work of between *nine and ten thousand* full time staff under (a) above alone***.

Costs of treatment

Turning to the costs of treatment, it is officially estimated that over a tenth of district health authorities' expenditure is on services for people suffering from mental ill health, three quarters of whom are estimated to be of working age[3]. NHS employees (some 900,000, full and part time in England) account for some 3% of the total of those of working age. It is therefore clear that the NHS spends a not inconsiderable amount of its resources providing services for its own staff who develop mental health problems.

Thus both for humanitarian reasons, and for the very practical reasons of maximising output and, wherever possible, preventing calls on NHS services, the NHS has a keen interest in conducting itself as an employer in ways that sustain and promote the mental health of its employees.

What can the NHS do to promote the mental health of its employees

What can the NHS, or any other employer, actually do to try to sustain and promote the mental health of its employees? The basic difficulty in answering this is, of course, our limited understanding of the nature and causes of mental ill health. We are faced with a very wide range of conditions, for many of which causation remains disputed[4].

*** A note on how this estimate has been derived forms an annex to this paper.

But two things seem to be sufficiently clear to form the basis for practical action. In particular:

> first, there seems to be wide agreement[5] that many forms of mental ill health seem to be triggered by events or pressures outside the individual;

> second, it seems clear that exposure to such events or pressures does not always lead those concerned to suffer mental ill health. Neither being involved in a trauma such as a major accident, nor being under pressure due to long hours of work, sustained over long periods of time, seem themselves to be a sufficient condition for causing mental ill health[6]. The key thing seems to be the relationship between the external events or pressures and what might be described as the general state of the individual's mental health.

What causes one person to grow up with what might perhaps be called robust mental health, while others grow up with more fragile mental health, is a complex and disputed area, though agreement on the significance of the nature of the individual's earliest experiences would no longer be confined to those working in the psycho-analytic tradition. These matters are outside the scope of this paper. Rather, starting from the two base points set out above, we want to outline what might be done in relation to the events and pressures at work which can impair employees' mental health.

Our starting point is practical experience, supported by a wealth of research[7], of the central role *work* plays in many people's lives. For work is not simply how people earn the money to live. It is how we spend up to a third of our lives and to a considerable extent achieve our social and economic status. The opportunities we have at work and how fairly we are treated, are therefore major issues. 'Abuse' at work, which can arise in a variety of ways, may leave many employees apparently unaffected. But for others, it triggers mental ill health in one form or another[8].

What do we mean by 'abuse'? Essentially creating, or allowing to develop, working conditions which put people into avoidable traumatic situations or under quite unreasonable pressures. By way of example, there are the very practical issues of appointing people to particular posts, and induction arrangements.

If a manager gets it wrong, and appoints someone to a post who has insufficient basic capability, skill or experience for the work, the result soon shows in terms of sub-standard performance. What happens if this continues, despite the efforts of managers to help the individual concerned, by monitoring, arranging special training and so on? Sometimes the individual is dismissed: potentially a traumatic event for that individual and his or her family. All too often, perhaps especially in the public sector, the organisation accommodates to that sub-standard performance. Managers find ways of coping, by re-assigning tasks, or perhaps working around the under-performer and dealing directly with his or her sub-ordinates. Either way, the situation is one of potential stress – the trauma of dismissal, or the long term pressure on the individual of having it pointed out daily by the contrivances of his or her manager and other staff that he or she is not up to the job.

The results when someone is not up to the job to which he or she is appointed are well recognised – 'failing to deliver the goods' for the organisation and stress for the individual. What is perhaps less well recognised are the results where the work required in a post is not sufficiently stretching. For the organisation, there can be inefficiency because the individual is not properly engaged, and disruption as he or she tries to annex or create work inappropriately. For the individual, the result can be sustained boredom and, if there is no prospect of moving on to work of appropriate level, this itself can be destructively stressful.

Either way, therefore, management failure properly to match the capabilities of individuals to the requirements of particular jobs has the potential to put the individuals concerned under stress. And for a proportion of these the outcome will be a breakdown, or some other form of mental ill health.

Similar consequences apply in relation to induction arrangements. For example, nearly half of the NHS's workforce consists of nursing staff and traditionally the bulk of new entrants are young women leaving school. Their training on the wards brings them into intimate contact with serious illness, physical disability, mental disturbance and death, and the suffering that acocmpanies them. For some, these will be new experiences; for many, the scale of the experience can be overwhelming and immensely stressful.

How individual nurses react depends partly on the robustness of their mental health, but partly upon the adequacy of the induction and support arrangements that responsible managers create, or fail to create. Without adequate arrangements – both for initial induction and continuing oversight – there is the risk of breakdown for the individual, or the development of defences to the anxieties generated which may not be in the patient's best interests[9].

These two issues – appointments and induction arrangements – are but examples of the general point that the ways in which work is organised can have potent effects of the mental health of the individual employee. *All* aspects of the organisational arrangements and management practices contribute to creating work settings that either re-enforce good mental health among employees or to a greater or lesser extent threaten it.

If this view is accepted, the inescapable consequence for chief executives and others in senior managerial positions is that they have a responsibility which, depending on how it is discharged, may either sustain and enhance the mental health of their employees, or damage it. In either case there will also be an effect – good in the former, adverse in the latter – on the effectiveness of their organisations. For it will be noticed from the examples given of appointments and induction arrangements that the circumstances most conducive to sustaining or enhancing the individual's mental health are those which are most conducive to good organisational performance.

For any chief executive who shares this view, there is thus both a moral and a practical requirement to seek to institute organisational arrangements and management practices which provide a context in which each and every employee can use his/her capability, skills and experience to the full, and do not subject employees to avoidable trauma or stress.

What does this mean in practice? In the case of the examples already given it means:

first, taking a good deal more trouble than is often the case when making appointments, *and* then accepting responsibility for our failures. If a manager makes a misjudgement, and appoints an immediate sub-ordinate who proves not to be quite up to the job, the manager should accept responsibility for his or her error of judgement. The proper response is then to seek to help the person appointed out of what to both parties is an unsatisfactory situation. Wherever practicable, this should mean identifying another post more suited to the individual's capabilities;

second, it means recognising that the work within some jobs involves experiences that are potentially very stressful to many individuals. The answer is not to seek to avoid responsibility by ignoring the stresses, or to compensate for any suffering caused through higher pay. Rather, the proper response is to recognise the potential problem and to try to create conditions which properly support staff in their work.

More generally, there is the need to think about all organisational arrangements and management practices from the point of view of their likely impact on staff. The aim must be to ensure that organisations are what has been described as philogenic in character, rather than paranoiagenic[10].

These matters are not always properly attended to in the NHS, any more than we suspect they are in most other employment contexts. Even where there is recognition of the potential significance of organisational arrangements on individuals, there is little in the way of rigorous and coherent studies of what constitutes satisfactory arrangements to guide managers.

Proposed testing of ideas

For this reason it is intended to undertake within the NHS systematic work, overseen by the Chief Executive personally, to test some very concrete ideas for organising work at hospital level which it is hoped will both result in substantial improvements in performance and go a long way to eliminating avoidable trauma or stress on staff. If these ideas are successful in practice, one consequence should be a reduction in absence due to mental ill health.

The work will be undertaken by the NHS Chief Executive's Policy Unit in collaboration with one or more NHS trusts or units managed by health authorities, using the general theory developed by Professor Elliott Jaques known as Stratified Systems

Theory[11]. It is expected that the work will begin during 1992. It will be systematically recorded and a description of the work, and the results, will be published.

A note on the estimate of working days lost to the NHS because of certificated mental ill health among staff

*   The Department of Employment's figures show that in 1989/90 about eighty million days certificated sick leave through mental ill health was taken by the total full time workforce of twenty two million people;

*   the NHS in England employed around 585,000 full time employees in 1990, 2.6% of the total of twenty two million;

*   on the assumption that the incidence of mental ill health is no less in the NHS than in the full time workforce as a whole, 2.6% of the total of eighty million days lost, or about 2.1 million days, would have been lost by the NHS workforce;

*   taking a full working year as approximately 220 working days, 2.1 million days equals about 9,500 full working years.

References

1. See, for example, Jenkins R., *British Journal of Industrial Medicine*, **42**, 147–154, 1985.

2. Much of the evidence about health service workers comes from America; see, for example, Rose K. D. and Rosow I., *Archives of General Psychiatry*, **29**, 800, 1973, and Colligan M J, Smith M J, and Hurrell J J, *Journal of Human Stress*, **3**, 34–39, 1977. But British studies confirm the high prevalence of mental ill health among health workers, for example, Murray R M, *British Journal of Psychiatry*, **131**, 1, 1977, and Ruanski J and Cybulska E, *British Journal of Hospital Medicine*, **33**, 90–94, 1985.

3. *Mental Illness – The Fundamental Facts*, the Mental Health Foundation 1990, second page 'Those Who Suffer From Mental Illness'.

4. See, for example, Newton J., *Preventing Mental Illness*, Routledge & Kegan Paul, 1988 and Bentall R., *Reconstructing Schizophrenia*, Routledge, 1990.

5. See, for example, the range of studies listed in Newton J., at 4 above.

6. See, for example, Paykel E. S., 'Recent Life Events in the Development of Depressive Disorders' in Depue R. A. (ed) *The Psychology of the Depressive Disorders*, Academic Press, 1979.

7. See, for example, the references quoted in Jaques E., *A General Theory of Bureaucracy*, Heinemann, 1976, chapter 1.

8. See, for example, Parkes K. R. *Journal of Applied Psychology*, **67(b)**, 784–79.

9. Menzies-Lyth I., 'The Functioning of Social Systems as a Defence Against Anxiety', 1959, reprinted in Menzies-Lyth I., *Containing Anxiety in Institutions*, Free Association Books, 1988.

10. By Jaques E., in *Requisite Organisation*, Cason Hall and Co., 1989, page pair 133.

11. See Jaques E., *Requisite Organisation*, at 10 above, and *Executive Leadership*, Blackwell, 1991.

9

CASE STUDIES IN STRESS

Roslyn Taylor

Introduction

The reasons why companies provide stress management programmes for their staff are many and varied. My contention is that this provision is often made in haste during a crisis and without any planning. Stress problems need to be researched, commitment from senior management sought and follow-up courses included if behaviour change is really desired. So much money is wasted by throwing inappropriate training at a problem.

I have researched numerous organisations and counselled many individuals so using some of these cases, let us explore stress in organisations and the possibility of an optimum process when planning interventions.

Definition of stress

For the purpose of this paper stress is defined as consisting of demands made upon us (Internally or Externally) which we perceive as exceeding our adaptive resources. If we try to cope and that is ineffective this gives rise to stress. If this stress is prolonged then lasting psychological and physical damage may occur.

Examples of referrals

When I was starting out as an independent psychologist 10 years ago, many companies would ask me to provide an hour's stress workshop for a conference or 'away day'. In the hope of whetting their appetite for more, I would comply only to find that further training was deemed unnecessary as they had now 'done stress'. So this fleeting stress visitation was used to silence staff complaints about pressure of work, which was certainly not the aim I had in mind.

Case A

My first example is a manufacturing company which was previously family owned, but has recently been acquired by a multinational corporation. The change in working practices and increased demands from head office, led the staff to ask for stress management courses to help them cope. After investigation, it appeared that in fact it was the communication systems which were not adequate for a modern organisation. There was little flow of information to the workforce and no participation in decision making. For example, when a meeting was held to air grievances, a member of staff complained there was no freedom of colour choice in company cars. Umbrage was taken by Senior Managers who decided then and there to stop the perk of company cars. Grievances were never aired again.

In the light of this punitive regime, no wonder stress was felt by the staff. To ensure a change of philosophy, I insisted that senior management attended the stress management seminars, and obtained some awareness of how their decision making affected staff morale.

Case B

My next referral example is of a micro electronics company who had a very caring philosophy and a history of empowering staff to make decisions. However the recession in world markets could not escape even them and they had to make approximately 200 staff redundant. This decision was made unilaterally by head office with no discussion as to the implementation. Management and staff are reeling not only from the loss of jobs but the very obvious change in company culture. But as a caring employer they have asked for a help line for counselling support both for those made redundant and for the staff who remain.

Case C

Sometimes in smaller businesses it is the chairman or managing director who is the catalyst in wanting stress management intervention. Walter was the owner of an engineering company that had swiftly grown in size under his tutelage. Unfortunately the perfectionism that made him successful when he started was becoming destructive to himself, his family and colleagues.

He rarely delegated decision making at work, as he always felt he knew best. Staff were undermined by his lack of trust in them and motivation was at a low ebb. His obessionality began to spread to his home life. His family had to take off their shoes when they entered the house and had to hang their coats in a specific ordered way. It was no wonder that he was experiencing chest pain and had undergone invasive medical tests for coronary heart disease before being referred to me. Not only did I have to help Walter change his attitude and learn to relax but also advise his employees on a strategy to assert themselves and handle Walter.

Case D

Very few companies tackle stress in a planned and preventative way. The exception is a processing plant. Their control room operators are responsible for keeping the plant going and for repairing any breakdowns. A shutdown could cost hundreds of thousands of pounds and also endanger lives. To be an operator is a prestigious position but the company recently noticed that some staff were reluctant to be promoted and some were becoming very stressed prior to their shift.

This organisation has decided to investigate the causes of stress fully. They also want to institute a counselling service and to set up stress mangement courses for all managers and technicians as part of the company's training programme.

Case E

Of course some organisations get it horribly wrong. One hotel chain had 3 managers die of heart attacks in one month during which there had been considerable re-organisation. They wanted a stress programme urgently as staff feared for their health. But as the furore died, the perceived need disappeared and nothing was done. They are of course just storing up problems for the future.

The perceived need for stress management

So in summary, companies ask for stress management because of:—

1 Staff complaints about stress.

2 Change that exceeds employee adaptive resources.

3 Trauma, ie, death of employees, stress related illness, redundancy etc.

4 Viewing stress management as a preventative tool in an overall training programme.

Stressors

Bupa's survey of 20 companies in 1987 (see figure 1) revealed that too much work and pressure to perform were the major stressors experienced.

Figure 1 *Causes of stress*

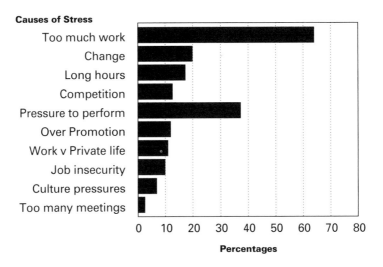

As a result of researching companies' stress problems, I have also noticed that overwork, with leaner staff and greater targets to reach, is a stressor. But boredom is also causing stress. Companies are still not utilising staff potential or rotating routine and repetitive tasks. A bored employee is not necessarily a bad employee. Increased responsibility can actually reduce stress and engender motivation. Unfortunately British managers still find a participative style a challenge. They are 'tellers' rather than 'askers' and organisations have a long way to go before staff feel involved in decision making. Lack of involvement in decision making, is today's major stress producer.

However, I wonder at the benefit of generalising at all about stressors as different organisations have very different reasons for experiencing stress. For example a group of financial services advisors (on commission only) reported that the pressure to earn every month, worry about their productivity and clients' cancelled appointments were for them major stressors. See figure 2 below.

Figure 2 *Stressors in study of financial services*

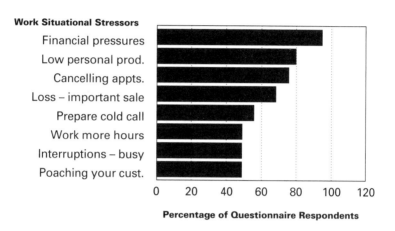

One particular consultant had only earned £59 that month and was extremely anxious not only about retaining his job but also his domestic survival. Sales training turned out to be more of a priority than stress management.

The Information Technology Department of a public company complained of feeling stressed because of recent changes. When the group was asked the cause, they reported a lack of managerial skills eg, the poor ability of managers to communicate and the absence of organisation skills. See figure 3 below.

The staff were all too aware of managers' deficiencies. One manager for example carried out an appraisal in the gents toilet which certainly annoyed the women. 'What do we have to do to be appraised?' they cried at one focus group. 'Hang around outside the gents or invite him to the loo next door?'.

Systems were there but managers did not have the people skills to carry them out properly. Managers themselves, who were adept technically were aware that handling staff, caused them headaches. Again stress management was lower down the list of

Figure 3 *Major stressors in a public organisation*

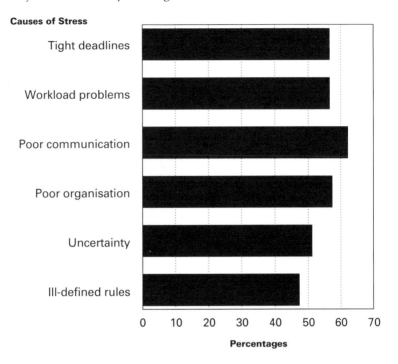

Figure 4 *Signs of stress noticed by managers – building society*

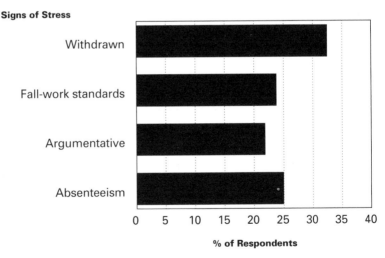

training priorities than self awareness training, assertiveness skills, positive thinking, problem solving or people management. See figure 5.

I must add that this organisation had been planning an expensive exercise programme for 50 staff costing £50,000. A proper analysis of the problem saved the company a considerable sum of money.

At an individual level proper analysis of difficulties is also important. The head of a new technology department became phobic about social encounters and was sent for help by his personnel officer. When analysed, his problem turned out to be a lack of training for the position he was now in. He had become a team leader, a liaison officer, a trainer and salesman in addition to being a technical expert. A two week managerial skills course restored his self confidence and his phobic anxiety disappeared. His recovery would have been less swift if his anxiety had been the only problem attended to.

These examples show that companies must make sure they get stress management counsellors and trainers with the requisite analytical skills. I would always suggest psychologists for this function because of their training in hypothesis testing in the field of behavioural analysis. Very few other professionals have the requisite skills and body of knowledge.

Signs of stress

Signs of stress may be different for each company. For example, managers of a Building Society noticed signs of withdrawal in their staff as being a significant sign of stress. See figure 4.

After training, it was interesting to note that their awareness had increased and more signs were noticed by managers than before, although stress in the organisation remained at the same level. They had by their own admission become more sensitive to staff problems.

Managers from a hotel chain were aware of high staff turnover as a sign of stress – some 200% a year in specific hotels. The worrying aspect for me was that this figure did not fill them with horror. If they had attended to staff needs, they might have retained them.

The Information Technology Department mentioned before had reported inter-departmental rivalry as a symptom of stress in their organisation. Staff also noticed that there was no follow through on projects. Everyone was so busy that nothing was ever completed. Come to think of it they also failed to follow through with any intervention after their stress management assessment.

One engineering company voiced its concern at the lack of participation at meetings. No-one disagreed with Senior Managers or even put their point of view. As a result they discovered machine prototypes in various parts of the factory with 'urgently needed for 1985' written on them (it was then 1990). Staff were failing to be assertive with managers about the viability of business targets. The company viewed this inhibition as a sign of stress and also bad management practice. This example shows that stress is simply not productive.

Interventions

I am a great believer in asking people themselves what interventions would make a difference to their working or domestic lives. The Information Technology Department who were going to have an exercise schedule inflicted on them, prioritised their needs efficiently, though I fear they never saw the results of their labours, see figure 5.

Figure 5 *Courses requested by respondents*

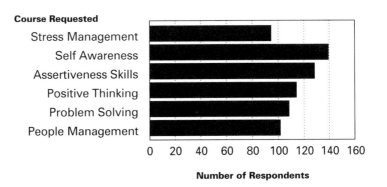

Stress management though seen as an important initiative was 6th on their list. Exercise did not feature as significant mainly because many staff had their own regimes already.

Guidelines for Interventions

1 Be it training or counselling any intervention must start with what will make a difference. If not staff will be disinclined to attend.

2   In addition my experience has shown that company personnel from the top down should go through the same training and as quickly as possible so that each level is rewarding and reinforcing the other's behaviour change.

3   Senior staff have to be involved because if employees became more assertive or talk more openly about their problems, it only takes one incident of repression through ignorance to ruin the complete investment in training.

4   Follow-up programmes are also crucial in making sure that the behaviour change as a result of a stress management intervention is not due to a workshop high. If participants know that they are going to be monitored then it sharpens their motivation to change, and maintain that change.

There are a whole range of interventions that might be necessary to help an organisation's stress problems. The combination will depend on the results of the initial research phase. A selection is listed below. See figure 6.

Figure 6 *Range of interventions*

Stress Management Courses

Relaxation Classes

Individual Counselling

Stress Watch Groups

Suggestion Schemes

Changes in Organisational Policy

Further courses that reduce stress

Time Management

Interpersonal Skills

Assertiveness Training

Exercise and Nutrition

Management Training

Team Building

Outcomes

A manufacturing company who instituted a communication skills and stress management programme throughout the organisation noticed the following changes as a result. See figure 7.

Figure 7 *Environmental changes*

Better Use of Space

Ventilation

Noise Reduction

Reduction of Open Plan

Health Promotion and Cafeteria Facilities Improved

Changes in communication

Team Briefings

Suggestion Schemes

More 'People Skills' Training

More dissemination of information

Understanding of the roles of others

More relaxed open management style

Like this company, many participants in Stress Management training comment on increased openness in relationships with colleagues, managers and subordinates, less vulnerabiity if they have to admit to feeling stressed and a greater understanding of personal wellbeing.

Northern Telecom, a telecommunications company in Northern Ireland is an example of an organisation which is dealing with stress in a planned way.

Cut backs and redundancies could have left staff stressed with morale at a low ebb, but the managing director planned a stress management programme prior to redundancy to help staff cope and recover. Managers, supervisors and operators were trained concurrently and follow up courses planned in advance.

Again a more relaxed open working environment with better relationships between levels was reported at follow up. It was also interesting to note that a large percentage of staff commented on increased personal development as well as work improvements. Of course the skills of handling stress are as applicable to home life as they are to the factory or office.

Another result of this study was the generation of a positive approach to the future of Northern Telecom and personal responsibility for the individuals' role in that future.

Much of the success of this programme is due to Ian Kennedy, the Managing Director. He was a 'training champion' who checked constantly on course feedback and personal change. In other words because of the speed of flow of information staff began to talk the language of stress management thus reinforcing each other's progress. While at the same time the Director was adding his stamp of authority thus giving the programme credibility.

This preventative approach which includes stress management as part of an overall training strategy where senior management actively backs the project, seems to work well.

Summary

It is best for a company to plan their stress management programme if they are going to confront stress properly, rather than play at it.

A suggested format is outlined in figure 8. Of course business needs change constantly so an annual stress check to reassess the situation helps an organisation to be appraised of any potential problems.

Conclusion

Stress needs to be taken seriously. If organisations wish to embark on stress management programmes they should follow a process of assessment, intervention and evaluation.

A short talk by an unskilled trainer will rarely provide the change needed for a less stressed, more productive organisation. Skills cost more but they are always worth it in the long run.

Reference

BUPA 1987, Stress survey of 20 companies. BUPA, Provident House, 24–27 Essex Rd., London.

FIGURE 8 *A Comprehensive Stress Management Programme Process*

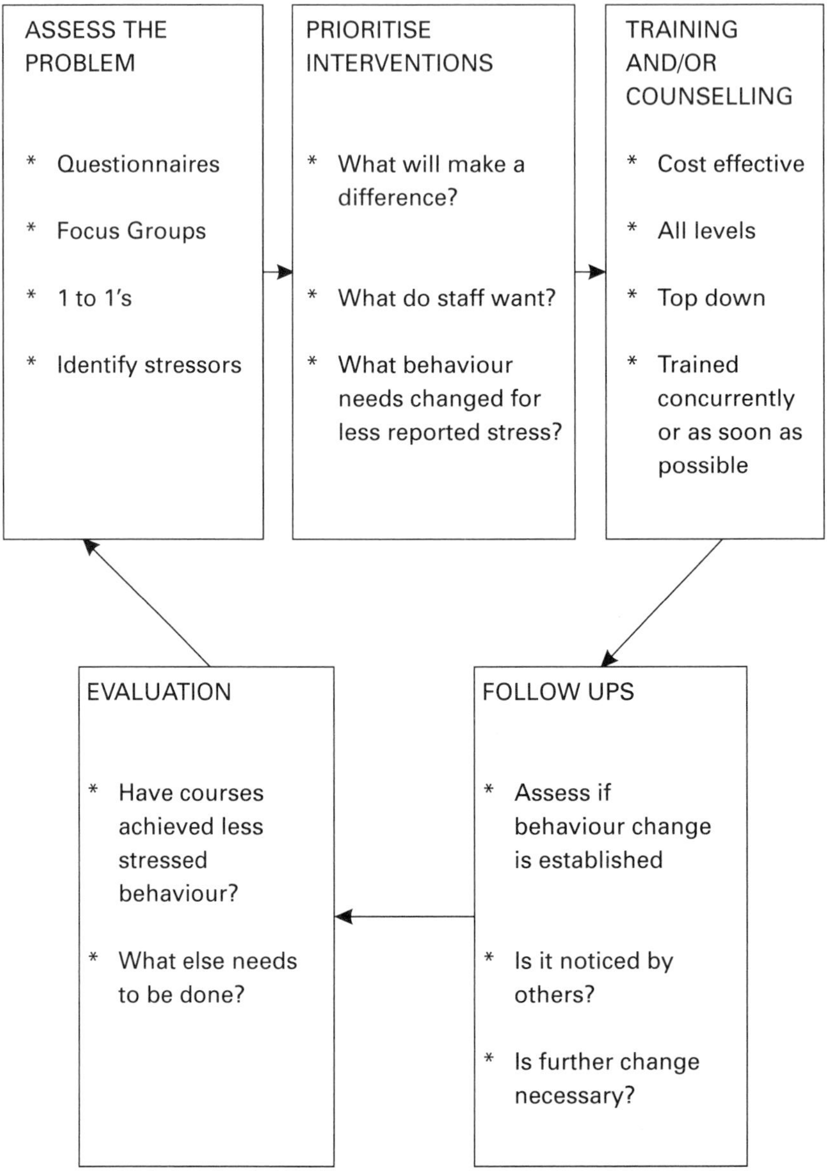

ASSESS THE PROBLEM	PRIORITISE INTERVENTIONS	TRAINING AND/OR COUNSELLING
* Questionnaires	* What will make a difference?	* Cost effective
* Focus Groups		* All levels
* 1 to 1's	* What do staff want?	* Top down
* Identify stressors	* What behaviour needs changed for less reported stress?	* Trained concurrently or as soon as possible

EVALUATION	FOLLOW UPS
* Have courses achieved less stressed behaviour?	* Assess if behaviour change is established
* What else needs to be done?	* Is it noticed by others?
	* Is further change necessary?

10

THE ROLE OF THE HEALTH AND SAFETY COMMISSION AND THE HEALTH AND SAFETY EXECUTIVE

Sir John Cullen, Chairman, Health and Safety

Commission

Introduction

Problems of mental ill health are widespread, and are likely to have some effect on most people at work. Most people will experience a mental health problem at some time, either in themselves or in a close colleague.

This can be costly to employers not only in terms of sick leave and staff turnover, but also in decreased productivity, and poor quality of work.

A key message is that people at work need to realise that problems of mental ill health are common, but that they are often of limited duration and can usually be treated. Some are preventable. Thus the stigma so often associated with mental ill health should go. One way is to regard mental health as a component of personal health, rather than as something separate and different[1]. Apprehension will diminish if that message is clearly understood.

The responsibilities of the Health and Safety Commission and The Health and Safety Executive

We can help in the Health and Safety Commission and the Health and Safety Executive. We have responsibility for the oversight of work-related risks to health and safety. The responsibility for managing these risks rests with employers and others at work. Our role is to propose legislation, codes and standards to ensure that action is actually taken to prevent accidents and disease. We promote compliance with the legislation not just by inspection and enforcement, but by providing advice and guidance. We also sponsor research, undertake investigations and collect information and statistics. These help us to identify the nature, scale and severity of hazards and risks. Different risks require different mixtures of these activities.

The Commission and its executive arm, the HSE, can become involved with mental health issues in all the activities I have just mentioned, for there are risks at work to mental as well as physical health. Mental health is covered by the general provisions of the Health and Safety at Work Act.

By way of example let me describe our involvement in two key areas:

- first, the provision of general guidance and advice, both published guidance, and face to face advice when our factory inspectors and other field staff meet employers and others in the workplace;

- second, our activities relating to the training and rehabilitation of those who have some kind of mental illness.

Guidance and advice: the need for policies on mental health

Our advice can be summed up as 'develop a policy'. We have produced a leaflet[2] that gives guidance on how to go about this and suggests the sort of topics that need to be considered. I expect that many organisations already have a policy on alcohol, but may not even have considered the possibility of having a policy on mental health. In today's uncertain and increasingly stressful environment, mental well-being is a crucial factor in economic well-being, particularly when the work activity of an employee is mental activity.

For many people work is a stimulating experience – and for most people it is probably an important factor helping to *avoid* mental health problems. But work can undoubtedly also cause stress and this can sometimes cause lasting ill health. There are no consistent data here, although surveys show that many employees consider that they suffer from stress at work. To find out more about those that *are* work-related we sponsored some research projects. Causation is nearly always complex, but even where it is external to the workplace it makes sense for employers to look for factors at work that might have an adverse effect on mental health problems as well as those that might be a risk to physical health; and to take appropriate action, particularly to reduce stress.

The way an organisation is structured, the way it communicates, and the way it treats individuals are all crucially important to the mental well-being of its employees. The need for good management has always been a cornerstone of our health and safety advice, and in recent years we have placed increasing emphasis on the need to pay regard to human factors and to establish effective risk assessment and control regimes. We believe and emphasize that most work-related accidents and ill health are preventable; that prevention is achieved through the systematic assessment and management of risk, and that this must be 'top down'. As in health and safety generally, it is essential for senior management to acknowledge that it is in their interests to promote health at work and to help prevent mental ill health.

Mental health policies will vary from one employer to another, but the basic principles will apply to all of them, whatever the size of the firm. They do not have to be long written statements but they should be an integral part of the organisation's policy on health and safety overall. They should cover the prevention of work-related stress, including ways in which the organisation will provide education and training, for example on stress management or the management of change; and what sort of help can be provided when needed – counselling, and helping an employee back to work after a period of sickness absence. It will be even more effective if the employer has a positive policy to provide good health including good mental health.

The costs of mental ill health are enormous. Making changes to existing systems may well cost money in the short term; but the benefits will accrue over time. Good health and profitability go together.

Recently, the Health and Safety Commission looked in depth at one occupation – school teaching – shown consistently in surveys to be particularly prone to stress at work. We produced a guide for managers and teachers on managing occupational stress[3]. The advice it contains is very much in line with Professor Cox's advice in Chapter 3 on developing control systems. Its messages about the control and prevention of problems in the education sector are relevant in many other areas of work.

Counselling, training and rehabilitation

No discussion on mental health can ignore counselling, an activity that has greatly increased in recent years. HSE is sponsoring a number of research projects to evaluate the effectiveness of counselling services. We hope this will help to answer some of the questions that are frequently put to our field staff by employers seeking advice.

Turning to rehabilitation, the Employment Medical Advisory Service, which is part of HSE and perhaps better known as EMAS, is a team of some one hundred doctors, nurses and others, trained and experienced in all aspects of occupational ill health. They are based in HSE's area offices. They provide professional help to the Careers Service and the Employment Service in the training and rehabilitation of people with health problems. A large proportion of the cases they see involve some form of mental health impairment. EMAS are also there to help employers, not by providing direct medical services, but by giving advice, for example on what occupational health provision is appropriate for an organization.

But rehabilitation is not just a matter for EMAS; employers and colleagues at work must also play their part. The patient undergoing treatment may or may not still be working. If working, employers may need to make adjustments to work loads or hours of work, and be generally supportive – not just for altruistic reasons, but because it makes good business sense. As for any employee returning to work after sickness absence, the employer will have to consider whether any factors related to work played a part in mental ill health leading to sickness absence. Timely modification of anything in the workplace that could be seen as a contributory cause of an illness can help facilitate the return to work, and improve work performance and productivity.

While considering the kind of short-term problems of mental ill-health that any of us might suffer we must not overlook the needs of those who have more serious, long-term conditions.

Some patients may need continuing treatment whether in or out of work; some may need to take medication for life – but in many cases this is by no means a barrier to full employment.

Conclusions

Mental illness can affect anyone. It need not and should not be a barrier to employment when staff are recruited or when employees who have been unwell return to work. Functional effectiveness for the job is what is important, not a past history which may include an illness where stigma outweighs knowledge.

With appropriate management systems mental ill-health can be minimised or controlled.

References

1 LUCAS G: Mental health at work, *Employment Gazette*, Dec 1989 **97** (12) 652–656.

2 The Education Service Advisory Committee of the Health and Safety Commission: *Managing occupational stress: a guide for managers and teachers in the schools sector*, HMSO, 1990, ISBN 0 11 885559 X.

3 The Health and Safety Executive: *Mental health at work*, reprinted December 1990. (IND (G) 59L: available free of charge from HSE).

Printed in the United Kingdom for HMSO
Dd297610 11/93 C7 G531 10170